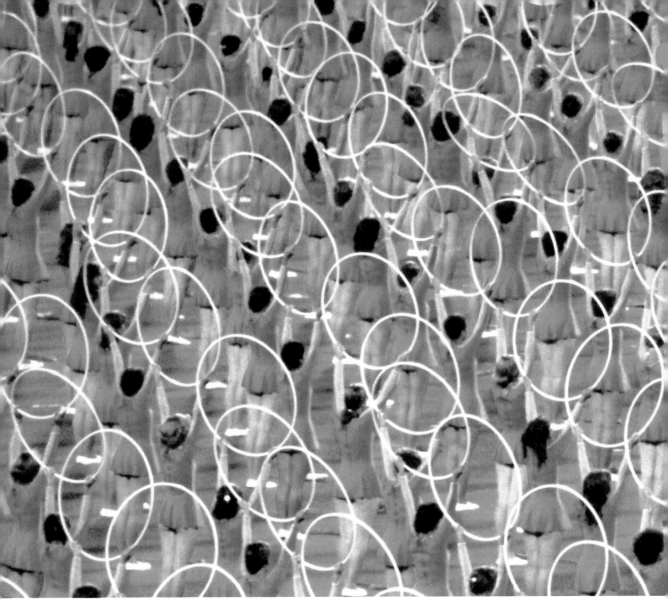

Introduction by James A. Michener

Olympic

Universe
in association with
Eastman Kodak Company

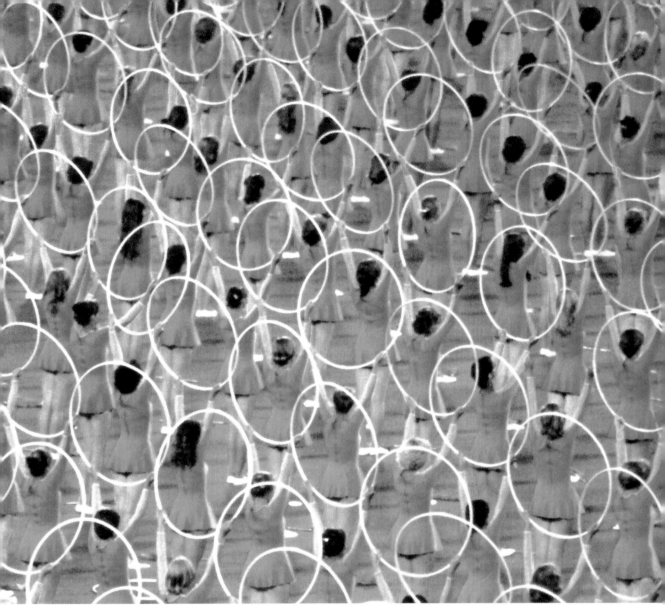

Douglas Collins

Dreams

U S A

LENCE 100 YEARS OF EXCELLENCE 100 YEARS OF EXCELLENCE 100 YEARS OF EXCELLENCE 100 YEARS OF EXCELLENCE 1

First published in the United States of America in 1996 by
UNIVERSE PUBLISHING
A Division of Rizzoli International Publications, Inc.
300 Park Avenue South
New York, NY 10010

Design by Mirko Ilić

Charts by Nigel Holmes

Library of Congress Card Catalog Number: 95-62466

Universe Publishing is an official licensee of the U.S. Olympic
Committee. The use of Olympic-related marks and terminology is
authorized by the USOC pursuant to Title 36 U.S. Code Section 380.

This book is dedicated to the members of the nearly victorious
1955 Wildcat team.

Printed in the United States of America

ACKNOWLEDGMENTS

The publisher is indebted to the principal contributors as well as to many other individuals for their extraordinary behind-the-scenes contributions and dedicated efforts. At the United States Olympic Committee, special gratitude is due to John Krimsky, Jr., Barry King, C. Robert Paul, Becky Baranyk, Cindy Slater, Pat Olkiewicz and Gigi Zvonkovich. For the Eastman Kodak Company's committed support, enormous thanks are due to Michael More and to Roland Schindler and Bill Benedict. At the Allsport photography agency, great appreciation is extended to Susan Baldus and Darrell Ingham as well as to researchers Paul J. Sales, Paul J. Prowse, Tony Graham and Val Ching. Michael Salmon of the Amateur Athletic Foundation was instrumental in obtaining rare photographs. Nigel Holmes brought this book's statistics to life with his charts and graphics. At Universe and Rizzoli, special thanks are offered to Antonio Polito, Bonnie Eldon, Jen Bilik, James Stave and Elizabeth White as well as to Olga Lamm, David McAninch, Karla Eoff and Beverly Fazio Herter. Finally, Mirko Ilić's vital design has resulted in a timelessly stylish book, a worthy showcase for the Olympic Games in all their glory.

OPENING CAPTIONS

Page 1: Opening ceremony, 1984. **Pages 2–3:** Opening ceremony, 1980. **Pages 4–5:** Opening ceremony, 1980. **Pages 6–7:** Opening ceremony, 1988. **Pages 8–9:** Opening ceremony, 1992. **Pages 10–11:** Opening ceremony, 1988. **Pages 12–13:** Summer Sanders (USA), 1992. **Pages 14–15:** Christine Klump (GER), 1992. **Page 16:** Heptathlon hurdlers, 1992. **Page 17:** Swimming start, 1992. **Page 18:** Diving over Barcelona, 1992. **Page 21:** Olga Korbut (SOV), 1972. **Pages 22–23:** Water polo match, 1992. **Pages 24–25:** Long jump, 1984. **Pages 26–27:** Seolla Umoh (CAN), 1992. **Pages 28–29:** Florence Griffith-Joyner (USA), 1988. **Page 30:** Lightweight judo, 1992. **Page 31:** Wrestling, 1992. **Page 32:** Solomon Amegatcher (GHA), 1992. **Page 33:** Tony Campbell (USA), 1992. **Pages 34–35:** Ernesto Aguero (CUB), 1992. **Pages 36–37:** Christian Schenk (GDR; standing), 1988. **Pages 38–39:** Mary Lou Retton (USA), 1984. **Page 40:** Trent Dimas (USA), 1992. **Page 41:** Waldemar Malak (POL), 1992.

TABLE OF CONTENTS

100 YEARS OF EXCELLENCE 100 YEARS OF EXCELLENCE 100 YEARS OF EXCELLENCE 100 YEARS OF EXCELLENCE 100 YEARS OF EXCE

OLYMPIC VISIONS

Photography has stood at the side of the Olympic Games from the very first days of this burgeoning international athletic phenomenon, functioning to record the spectacle, memorialize athletic achievements and spread the Olympic message around the globe. By the time of the games of the first Olympiad in Athens in 1896, the Eastman Kodak Company had been producing photographic products for about seventeen years. But such was the practically instantaneous worldwide acceptance of George Eastman's revolutionary roll-film system that by the turn of the century Kodak cameras were in hundreds of thousands of hands and Kodak outlets had been opened in many parts of the world—one of which, coincidentally, was Athens, Greece.

In 1908 the Olympic Games were held in London. One of the most enthusiastic supporters of Kodak roll-film photography in the country happened to be the Queen of England, who was an avid amateur photographer herself and who had earlier granted George Eastman a warrant as purveyor of photographic materials to the royal family. Perhaps owing to her official duties, Queen Alexandra apparently did not have the chance to take any Olympic photographs, though given her prodigious output of pictures, it is easy to imagine that she would have loved to do so. Alexandra was there when, directly in front of the royal box, one of the most famous pictures in Olympic history was taken: Italian marathoner Dorando Pietri's collapse into the arms of officials as he stumbled across the finish line.

In 1912 the Swedish Organizing Committee turned to photography for more than great images. Officials realized that referees, though trained and experienced, sometimes had difficulty calibrating the very small intervals separating runners at the tape. What could better help than a photograph, which officials could pass around and discuss and which would provide convincing proof to athlete and spectator alike? First used to sort out finishers in both the 800- and 1,500-meter races in 1912, finish-line photography has since been a staple of the Olympics, and our company has been a prime contributor.

Another category of technological change, though less noticeably spectacular, has had a huge overall effect on the spread of Olympic images: the progress made in photofinishing during the past one hundred years. Since 1888, Kodak photofinishing technology has made it look easy. Before roll film, glass plates had to be painstakingly developed in multiple chemical solutions—no job for an amateur. With the introduction of the first Kodak camera, photographers had only to send the film and cameras back to the Kodak laboratories, wait about three weeks, and have a set of finished prints returned by mail.

By the time the one-hundredth anniversary of the Olympic Games is celebrated in Atlanta, Kodak will have introduced a new photographic system: By means of information coded upon the film, seventeen computers in our new photoprocessing units will be able to make 2,500 calculations per negative and still produce four prints per second. With the first Kodak camera the company promised, "You push the button, we do the rest." If the photographer took a poor picture, however, there was little we could do to fix it. With our new system, you still push the button, but even if the shot is not perfect, Kodak will go a long way toward producing a better photo.

Only sixteen years ago, our photo laboratory at the Lake Placid Winter Games was set up in an old schoolroom and was serviced by a mere handful of technicians. In Atlanta our facility will comprise 20,000 square feet to house several hundred experts. Rather than simply processing pictures and packing them for delivery in courier bags, these experts will scan images on computers and transmit the pictures' digitized versions all over the world for immediate consumption.

Today Kodak is proud to be an official sponsor of the Olympic Games, and we look forward to continuing our longtime partnership with the Olympic movement. As the following pictorial history suggests, these one hundred years have been dramatic and fruitful for both of us. If history is any guide, it can be certain that in coming years we at Kodak, along with our Olympic colleagues, will continue to raise the bar every chance we get.

George M. C. Fisher
Chairman, President and Chief Executive Officer, Eastman Kodak Company

OLYMPIC CENTURY

The athletes pursuing the Olympic dream represent the future of our nation and stand for what is best in the world of sport. It is the athletes we have come to know and respect who have given the Olympic movement its unique integrity for the past one hundred years. The sight of such men and women as Dan Jansen, Janet Evans and Michael Johnson doing extraordinary things on the field of play is our fundamental motivation for being involved in, promoting and memorializing the Olympics.

The United States Olympic Committee was inaugurated on November 21, 1921, for the same reason that it exists today: to serve the dreams and ambitions of American Olympians. First based in New York City, the organization that came to be known as the U.S.O.C. has counted among its ranks some illustrious characters, among them sports magnate A. G. Spalding and future military legend General Douglas MacArthur (each served as president of the organization during its early years). Today, the United States Olympic Committee is a vast, multifaceted organization representing the interests of nearly 42 million sports people. Working closely with national sports federations and the International Olympic Committee, the U.S.O.C. functions first and foremost to provide American athletes with the guidance and material support they need to be the best, both in the Olympic venue and beyond.

U.S.O.C. programs provide support to thousands of athletes each year; the skier Chris Waddell is one of them. Chris was paralyzed below the waist in a 1988 skiing accident, but his desire to compete coupled with the support of the United States Olympic Committee led to his winning four gold medals at the 1994 Paralympic Winter Games.

10

Other athletes benefit directly from the U.S.O.C.'s grant program, which awarded approximately 10,000 grants worth more than $26 million during the four-year period leading up to the 1996 Olympics. Additionally, the United States Olympic Committee remains firmly devoted to the interests of the thousands of non-professional athletes who depend on U.S.O.C. support. The U.S.O.C.–sponsored Olympic Job Opportunity Program has helped athletes like the diver Mary Ellen Clark, a 1992 bronze medalist. Mary Ellen is one of 441 athletes who have been able to benefit from solid work experience while continuing their athletic careers thanks to the program's job-placement services. The U.S.O.C. also provides material support to athletes in the form of facilities, such as the all-weather A.R.C.O. Training Center in Chula Vista, California. A total of 20,000 athletes pass through the doors of the Olympic training centers in Chula Vista, Colorado Springs and Lake Placid each year.

The United States Olympic Committee has, like the Olympic movement itself, grown immensely over the years, both in its size and in the breadth of its commitments to the athletes who are its most important clients. It is our ultimate goal that the U.S.O.C.'s impressive growth will continue to yield the one dividend that is the true measure of its success: the realization—for thousands of young athletes—of the Olympic dream.

Dr. LeRoy T. Walker
President, United States Olympic Committee

11

INTRODUCTION

When Baron Pierre de Coubertin, a French sportsman, had the brilliant idea of reinstituting the Olympic Games, which had last been held in ancient Greece in 393 B.C., he insisted that they be held in Greece, and in 1896 they were. A huge emotional and sporting success, they were from the beginning an international celebration, with athletes from thirteen nations participating.

Many experts, thinking mainly of past history rather than contemporary reality, proposed that a stadium be built in Greece in which the games would be held every four years, as in the old days. But Coubertin visualized a much better system. To ensure the continuance of their international flavor, he proposed that the site of the new games be changed every four years to a new nation, and in 1900 the games were held in Paris, which was a much weaker show. The 1904 games were held in St. Louis, a performance even sloppier than the one in Paris, and there was serious talk of abandoning the games as an idea that had been vital at the start but had no staying power.

I have been in love with the Olympic movement since I was old enough to comprehend what internationalism meant as a unifying concept, and those exciting days when I became familiar with the colorful athletes of so many different nations. The Montreal Olympics of 1976 were the only ones I would attend in person, but since they were less than a day's drive from my home, I felt I had to look in, and it was thus that I saw Nadia Comaneci earn some of her perfect 10s. Like so many other witnesses, I was breathless as she went through her routines, and I agreed with the Canadian sitting next to me when he said reverently: "She's like the queen of the elves." As I followed the games I saw that they fell into different levels of excellence and that they enjoyed not only years of triumph, but also decades of decadence and even tragedy. I have categorized these sometimes overlapping epochs as follows:

Fumbling About. After 1896, the games were held in cities ill-prepared to host such important international spectacles, and during several points of conspicuous decline it was proposed that the quadrennial competition be terminated. But the directors of the games and the athletes persisted in striving to continue the Olympics in a progressively revitalized form.

Golden Age I. These were the years when I first became aware of the grandeur of the games. I was old enough to appreciate the magnificence of the preparations, the pageantry of the surroundings in cities like Amsterdam, Berlin, Helsinki and Melbourne, and even more important, the parade of great world-class athletes: Paavo Nurmi, the Finnish distance runner; Charley Paddock, the American sprinter; Emil Zátopek, the Czech runner; Lord Burghley, the handsome British hurdler; and Valery Brumel, the taciturn Soviet high jumper. The age was made more golden by the performances of America's great black athletes, such as Jesse Owens who humbled Hitler in Berlin in 1936. The age was also graced by the exciting performances of women athletes who often dominated the news: Fanny Blankers-Koen, the Dutch housewife who won a score of medals in the Olympics and the national and European championships; the awesome Babe Didrikson, who excelled not only in everything Olympic but also in baseball, basketball and golf; and Wilma Rudolph, an American who overcame childhood polio to win three gold medals as a superb speedster. But the delightful highlight of the Golden Age was the dazzling appearance of amazing girl gymnasts: Olga Korbut, a seventeen-year-old from Byelorussia, who came on the Olympic scene in 1972, setting the stage for those who would follow; Nadia Comaneci from Romania; and Mary Lou Retton from West Virginia—three young princesses who won the hearts of the entire world.

But over the games of the Golden Age loomed the Herculean figure of a college student, the incredible Al Oerter, who would accomplish what no other athlete would achieve in modern times: win the gold in his favorite track event, the discus, in four successive Olympics—1956 in Melbourne, 1960 in Rome, 1964 in Tokyo and 1968 in Mexico City. He was a mighty man.

The Turbulent Times. I followed the games intimately during this unhappy spell, which included a boycott by the African nations and the United States Olympic Committee's decision not to send its athletes to the Moscow Games of 1980. I was infuriated by the anti-American judging in boxing and gymnastics. I studied also how the Communist nations shamelessly ignored the tradition that the games were for amateur athletes, and I watched with a mixture of repugnance and envy as the East German republic brazenly sent to the Olympics young super-athletes who had been paid with government funds. In these years the East German athletes won a surprising number of medals, especially those big, powerful women, some of whom were suspected with good reason of substance abuse.

But those offenses paled beside the personal tragedies that came in such volume and speed to make many critics wonder if the games did not do more harm than good. In the 1984 Olympiad, held in Los Angeles, the American favorite, a promising young woman named Mary Decker, was well on her way to winning the 3,000-meter race when she collided from behind with Zola Budd, the South African woman running for Britain, and fell crashing onto the cement curb marking the inside of the track. Her fall was so heavy and uncontrolled that she was unable to rise, let alone try to finish the race. Her illustrious career was damaged and Zola Budd saw hers contaminated in the newspaper warfare that followed. In time Mary made a partial recovery in the field of women's racing, but Zola never did—at least as far as the media was concerned. One of the causes of the bad press was that she had started as a citizen of South Africa, picked up her Great Britain passport and then reverted to her South African one. She was a dear, quiet girl who was treated abominably by the press but retained her dignity to the end.

Equally controversial was the case of the black American sprinters Tommie Smith and John Carlos in the 1968 Mexico City Olympics. When they won the gold and bronze medals in the 200-meter footrace, and mounted the podium to receive their medals while the band played "The Star Spangled Banner," they did not listen reverently but instead raised clenched fists as a sign of Black Power and a criticism of race relations in the United States.

Somewhat less political was the case of the sprinter Ben Johnson, a speedster born in Jamaica but now with Canadian citizenship. He and many of his countrymen believed him to be the fastest runner in the world. He seemed to excel in all aspects of the race: he got out of the blocks with a tremendous burst of speed, he ran superbly in the middle part and exploded at the finish. His adversaries, pointing to his massive musculature, accused him of taking steroids to augment his powers, but he and his coach, a Canadian expert, denied the accusation. Johnson further damaged his reputation by boasting: "When the gun goes off, the race is over."

Johnson was an accurate predictor, for when the starting gun went off in the Olympics the race was indeed over, and all Canada exulted in his bold victory. But things began to unravel: steroid tests proved that Ben had taken copious doses. A great scandal followed, and Johnson was deprived of his gold medal and banished from international competition.

Of true Homeric tragedy of course were the events that stained the Berlin Olympics of 1972, when eight Palestinian terrorists infiltrated the Olympic Village, located the dormitory where the Israeli team was sleeping and killed two Israelis instantly, taking nine others hostage. In the gun battle that ensued, the Palestinians shot each of the hostages at point-blank range. The games were suspended for thirty-four hours, and the joyousness that usually accompanied the Olympics was soured.

The Golden Age II. Yet at the close of the Moscow Games in 1980 I felt the Olympics had entered a new stage of grandeur and propriety, despite the Soviet boycott in 1984. I wish that the publishers of this book could at this point arrange for a bevy of trumpeters to sound a fanfare, a battery of guns to fire a salute, fireworks to brighten the sky and a mixed chorus to sing appropriate words to the final movement of Beethoven's Ninth. I want to do this to celebrate the 1992 games in Barcelona that were near perfection. They brought grace and significance to the Olympic idea and I hope the city fathers of Atlanta have Kodachrome slides of the Barcelona celebration because for us to equal or surpass that, the people of Atlanta had better be on their toes.

James A. Michener
Texas Center for Writers, January 1996

PREFACE

Though his labors numbered ten, not the twelve attributed to legendary Olympics founder Hercules, late in the gloomy evening of August 6, 1948, a cold, wet, exhausted seventeen-year-old American named Bob Mathias finally completed his Herculean tasks. "Never," the latest winner of the Olympic decathlon said to himself, "will I do this again."

This pledge, understandably uttered after two days of bone- and brain-wearying athletic exertion, was eventually broken. Mathias did train for another Olympic decathlon and, like Hercules, whose mythical accomplishments were chronicled in twelve metopes on the temple at Olympia, Mathias added to his fame with further exploits. In 1952 he won a second consecutive title, this time by a record-breaking margin of 800 points.

The obvious question, one that can be asked of all Olympic competitors, is: Why? What powerful enticement compels athletes to spend years preparing for the games? What, besides a small gold medal and, in comparison to other sports, relatively short-lived fame, is the attraction? Why would all agree with the statement attributed to a friend of an ancient Olympic champion who said, "Die, Diadorus, for thou has nothing short of divinity to live for"?

Though these questions can perhaps finally be answered only by the athletes themselves, it is clear that the historical character of Olympic competition contributes a distinct and special magnetism to this unequalled sporting event. Though Olympic recordkeeping began only in 776 B.C., when Coreobus of Ellis won the one-stade (200-meter) race, it is probable that athletic contests had long been held at the sacred site of Mount Olympus. Historians argue about the precise correlation between sports and spirituality, but it is clear that Greek civilization understood

the link as the human responsibility to perform godlike feats in an arena that was watched over by the gods themselves. Training for the games was considered an ethical, reverential, even devotional duty. "If you have been guilty of no slothful or ignoble act," the ancient competitors were told prior to competition, "go on with courage. You who have not so practiced, go wither you will."

Though the games were clearly vital to the Greek spirit, they were also great fun. Religious ritual coexisted quite comfortably with pure, crowd-pleasing spectacle. As such, the games grew in breadth and stature. Over time, new events were added to complement the one-stade race: the diaulos (double course), the dolichos (long footrace), the pentathlon (broad jump, javelin, discus, one-stade race and wrestling) and the pankraton (combined boxing and wrestling). This last event was fairly brutal, basically a no-holds-barred brawl that resulted in at least one death. In an effort to free himself from a chokehold, a fighter named Arrachion broke one of his opponent's toes. In extreme pain, the fellow raised his hand in defeat. At precisely the same moment, Arrachion, still unable to breathe, died. Since victory was ascertained by a signal of defeat, Arrachion, though dead, was named that year's pankraton champion.

The ancient Olympics were, not surprisingly, all-male events. Women were forbidden even to attend, which prompted at least one attempt to circumvent the prohibition. Phernice of Rhodes, who had helped to train her son Pisidore as a boxer, so wanted to see him compete that she disguised herself as a man to enter the games. When Pisidore won, his mother became so excited that she dislodged her cloak while rushing to congratulate him,

31

disclosing her identity and her gender. Though Phernice was not executed, as was the prescribed penalty, women generally remained absent throughout the early history of the games. A few women, such as Cyniska of Sparta, were awarded victory wreaths, though these were given in absentia and only because the women owned winning chariots.

The Olympic Games continued to be held every four years even after Greece had lost its world primacy to the Roman Empire. But the spirit was gone, and the games reached their all-time low when the Roman emperor Nero attended and indeed entered a number of events, all of which were rigged in his favor. After years of this kind of inattention to the high state of the Olympics, the games were finally discontinued by Emperor Theodosius in A.D. 393. The decline, initiated by time and politics, was ultimately concluded by natural forces such as earthquakes, and within a very short time the stadium and temple at Olympia were in ruins.

It is not clear how much detailed information the Frenchman Baron Pierre de Coubertin knew about the ancient Olympics, but in general he had the idea right. Coubertin was concerned about the state of contemporary education, in particular its inability to combine mental and physical exercise in a broad and international way. A revival of the Olympic Games, he thought, would be the perfect vehicle to carry his educational reforms to fruition. In pursuit of this ideal, Coubertin called an international sports congress, held in Paris in 1894, and plans were made to hold the first of the revived Olympic Games in Athens in 1896.

By the measure of more recent games, this first revival was poorly attended. But the question must again be

asked: Why did even those few who traveled to Athens come at all? Because of the belief in Courbertin's Olympic ideal? Probably not. It is more likely that the main motivation was no different from the one that had impelled ancient Greeks: The athletes came for the victories they expected to win and for the glories they hoped to attain.

Not all that stands between the athletes and their dreams shows up on the tracks or in the fields, stadiums and pools. Each team member represents and is represented by a National Olympic Committee. This means, first of all, that any individual athlete is not simply a runner, swimmer, soccer player or shot-putter. Specialties are always preceded by the name of a country; one is an American sprinter, a Swedish gymnast or a Kenyan marathoner. Second, each Olympic contestant more or less embodies his or her country's political philosophy and position in the world. Indeed, athletes have, as in 1980 and 1984, been unable to participate due to international disputes. Athletes are thus sometimes forced into awkward positions, the desire to compete conflicting with national policies.

Athletes have also been conflicted about the long-standing controversy over the difference between amateur and professional status. The issue first arose in Britain when the upper classes, not wanting to compete against the lower classes, maintained that those who worked, no matter what they did, were professionals. This tradition carried over through the early games, and evolved into an entrenched code against athletic professionalism. With the growing recognition of the reality of changes taking place in international sports, however, distinctions between amateur and professional status have been increasingly blurred.

Olympic athletes in ancient times were no less celebrated than in the modern era. The pankraton champion Poulydamas, who was undefeated in 1,400 contests, was certainly as renowned as the American hurdler Edwin Moses, who did not lose a race in over nine years of competition. And how dissimilar from the well-known and extremely colorful 1960 Olympic boxing champion Cassius Clay was Milo, the Greek wrestler, who in addition to competing in the Olympics performed such tricks as bursting a string tied around his forehead simply by straining and bulging his cranial veins?

Indeed, it seems fair to say that there has been very little fundamental change in the nature of athletic endeavor since 776 B.C. Though little anecdotal evidence remains about specific ancient events, one can easily imagine athletes from different parts of Greece finding themselves in rivalrous situations roughly equivalent to that of 1896 American hurdler Tom Curtis. Arriving at his Athens hotel, he was asked by the innkeeper about his specialty, and Curtis told the fellow that he was a hurdler. The Greek man responded with a sympathetic chuckle: "We have the best hurdler in the world." In fact, the innkeeper whispered, just recently this native runner had broken the 20-second mark. Curtis did not respond, keeping secret the fact that he routinely ran the 100-meter race in 18 seconds. The day of the final, the Greek runner was nowhere to be seen, having been eliminated in the heats. But Curtis had to deal with a similarly confident national champion, the British hurdler Grantley Goulding, who proudly showed Curtis all his accumulated medals. After being swept away at the end of the race, which Curtis won by a comfortable

margin, Goulding reportedly packed his bags and left Greece.

Even with all these intrigues and links between ancient and modern, still the question remains: Why do they come? Like Curtis, Goulding and the unidentified Greek, certainly, they come not simply to compete but to win. Can they all win? Of course not. In 1992, 9,300 athletes traveled to Barcelona with dreams of winning a gold medal in one of approximately 200 Olympic events. Inevitably, most of the competitors returned home with their dreams dashed. In other words, so few win gold medals as to make the possibility almost unthinkable to the majority of competitors.

To slightly invert the Olympic credo, is it better to lose than not to compete at all? By all historical evidence, that certainly seems to be true. Consider the case of the 1972 and 1976 Haitian entrants in the 10,000 meters. After Anilus Joseph began sprinting during the bell lap in the Munich race, the twice-lapped runner suffered the embarrassment of being told that he still had a mile to go. Joseph just walked off. Four years later his countryman Olmeus Charles suffered an even worse humiliation: He was so far behind that he ran the last six laps of the race entirely alone, finally finishing almost 9 minutes after the last runner had left the track.

Did these two come to lose? Not really, though they certainly knew they would be badly defeated. Did each harbor the slightest, the faintest, the most fleeting fancy that they might, just might win? Almost certainly. So they ran, that complex but compelling Olympic vision, the hope of victory mingling with the prospect of defeat, standing for them, as it had for thousands of others, as the Janus-like tutelary godhead from which all Olympic dreams descend.

35

1896 ATHENS 1896 **Urn carried from Temple of Jupiter to Temple of Hera, symbolically opening Olympic Games** ATHENS 1896 ATHENS 1896 ATHEN

Athens
1896

Ruins at Olympia

The first pop of an Olympic starting pistol was heard on April 6, 1896, by the more than fifty thousand enthusiastic spectators gathered in the huge new sports stadium constructed for the revived Olympic Games. This inaugural race, the first of three heats of the 100-meter sprint, was won by Francis Lane, an American collegian, in 12.6 seconds, a time that he repeated in the final, but which was then only fast enough to place him fourth. The other two 100-meter sprint heats run that morning were also won by Americans, Thomas Curtis and Thomas Burke—victories that quieted the predominantly Greek crowd, which was rooting for their champion, Alexandros Chalkonondilis.

Nor were the Greek fans any happier later that afternoon when another American athlete, James B. Connolly, won the triple jump and was awarded the first modern Olympic first-place medal. Connolly had been attending Harvard College when he heard about the renewal of Olympic competition. When his request for a semester's leave of absence to travel to Athens was turned down, he quit school and packed his bags.

Connolly's assurance and adventuresomeness extended to his competitive spirit. The last to compete in his event, he walked onto the field, tossed his cap a yard beyond the longest mark and then proceeded to leap over even that distance. The crowd, apparently delighted by both Connolly's feat and his on-the-field esprit, chanted, "Nike, nike," the Greek word for victory.

In many ways, the Greek hosts were as good sports and hosts as ever seen during the next hundred years. King George I, who had opened the games that morning surrounded by a formally attired diplomatic corps, was in

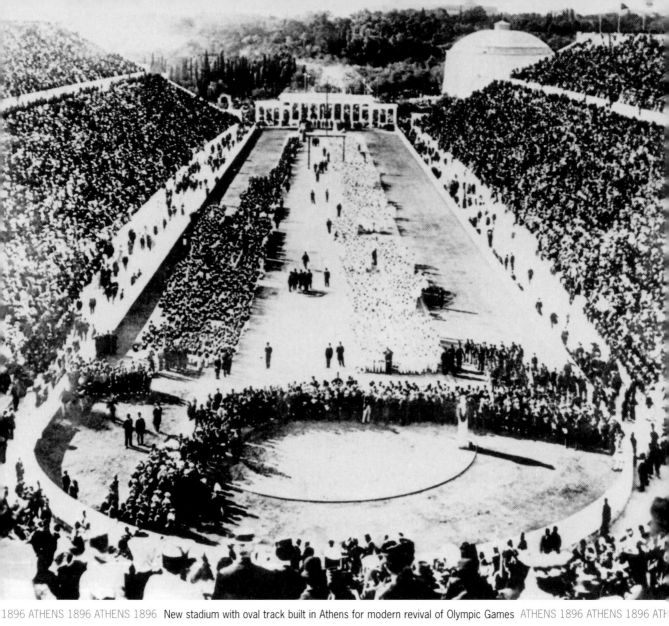

New stadium with oval track built in Athens for modern revival of Olympic Games

constant attendance. And though some athletes complained about the mushiness of the cinder track and its tight hairpin turns, the Olympic stadium, ringed by green hills, was itself beautifully designed. Indeed the first of the modern games, despite the breaking of a tie in the super-heavyweight weight-lifting contest by giving style points to Great Britain's Launceston Elliot, was conducted almost without complaint or controversy.

Even the swimming races, which were held in the 55-degree waters of the Bay of Zea at Phaleron, were contested with good nature by the freezing swimmers. The Hungarian Alfred Hajos, for instance, who had earlier won the 100-meter freestyle, painted his body with a half-inch thick layer of grease before the starting line of the 1,500-meter freestyle. As Hajos remembered, "I shivered from the thought of what would happen if I got a cramp from the cold water. But my will to live completely overcame my desire to win." Hajos swam on, blindly, and only upon reaching the mouth of the bay, noticing the boats rowing out past him to rescue other exhausted swimmers and hearing the roar of the seaside crowd did he realize he had "won ahead of the others with a big lead."

Thirteen nations sent teams to Athens, though the word "team" must be used loosely. Take the United States contingent, for instance, which was made up largely of members of the Boston Athletic Association, whose expenses were paid by the last-minute, private fund-raising effort of Oliver Ames, the former governor of Massachusetts. In this, the B.A.A. athletes were luckier than most. The majority of contestants, all of whom were male—this being the nineteenth century—paid their own way.

44

Team sent to Athens by Princeton University: F. A. Lane, A. C. Tyler, R. Garrett, H. B. Jamison

As it turned out the B.A.A., not the U.S.A., could be said to have been the great victor in 1896. Of the eight Boston athletes, six accounted for eight first-place victories, and the remaining two won seconds. Ellery Clark became the only man in Olympic history to score firsts in both the long and high jumps. Indeed, of the twelve track-and-field events, eight were won by multiple winners: the Australian runner Edwin Flack won the 800-meter race two days after defeating the American Arthur Blake in the 1,500-meter race, and the young Princeton track-and-field star Bob Garrett bested his Greek opponents in both the discus and shot put.

This is not to say that athletes from other countries all came up empty-handed. In the very popular cycling events, French, German and Austrian cyclists were consistent winners. The French also, along with Greeks, dominated the fencing matches. And in gymnastics, the Germans and the Swiss took the majority of medals.

The first, and perhaps sunniest of the modern Olympic Games ended on a hopeful, collegial and festive note. The day before, the patient Greek nation had achieved its great, awaited-for victory: the startling win in the marathon by the unknown Greek shepherd Spiridon Loues, who crossed the finish line flanked by the royal sons Prince George and Crown Prince Constantine. Buoyed by this triumph and by the overall success of the games, King George invited all 260 athletes and officials to a lavish, communal breakfast on the morning after the Olympics ended. After multiple toasts and many handshakes, Baron de Coubertin rose and declared the games a success, promising to continue the Olympic movement with greater and even more exciting events in the future.

Boston Athletic Association Olympians: Paine, Graham, Paine, Blake (seated); Burke, Curtis, Clarke (standing)

THOMAS BURKE

In 1896 international track-and-field competition did not exist in any real form. Athletes did not know what to expect from their competitors in times, distances and other measures of victory. National champions might completely overmatch other national champions. The Americans, for instance, were just as surprised by their dominance of the track-and-field events as were those they defeated.

Athletes and onlookers were also sometimes taken aback by styles and techniques. It seemed a revolutionary innovation to most when American sprinters assumed a crouched four-point stance at the starting line of the 100-meter sprint final. This technique apparently served the Americans well, as each 100-meter heat was won by a U.S. sprinter.

Speed, however, still counted above all. Thomas Burke repeated his 12.0 seconds heat time and beat his nearest competitor, the German Fritz Hoffman, by nearly 2 meters. (Hoffman's estimated time was 12.2 seconds.) The third, fourth and fifth runners were well behind, each finishing with an estimated time of 12.6 seconds. Burke was so fast and such a good athlete that even while running through the tortuous and sharply angled turns of the 400-meter race, he beat his American teammate Herbert Jamison by 13 meters.

In spite of all the athletic ability gathered at Athens the conditions could not really be called "Olympic," and few if any records were broken. For instance, the winning times of the 100 meters at the next two Olympics were a full second faster than Burke's time.

46

Two American runners in four-point stance at start of 100-meter race

TRACK-AND-FIELD RESULTS OF THE FIRST MODERN OLYMPIAD

100-Meter Run	T. Burke, U.S.A.	12.0 sec.		Running Broad Jump	E. Clark, U.S.A.	20' 9¾"
400-Meter Run	T. Burke, U.S.A.	54.2 sec.		Running High Jump	E. Clark, U.S.A.	5' 11¾"
800-Meter Run	E. Flack, Australia	2 min. 11.0 sec.		Hop, Step and Jump	J. Connolly, U.S.A.	45'
1500-Meter Run	E. Flack, Australia	4 min. 33.2 sec.		Shot Put	R. Garrett, U.S.A	36' 2"
110-Meter Hurdles	T. Curtis, U.S.A.	17.6 sec.		Discus	R. Garrett, U.S.A	95' 7½"
Pole Vault	W. Hoyt, U.S.A.	10' 9¾"		Marathon	S. Loues, Greece	2 hrs. 55 min. 20 sec.

Left: Marathon winner Spiridon Loues. Center: Finish of 1896 marathon.

MARATHON

The marathon, now so sentimentally associated with the Olympic Games, appears to have been a purely modern creation. Despite the fact that Baron de Coubertin and the initial Olympic organizing committee thought that a race based on Pheidippides's legendary, and probably mythical, 490 B.C. run to Athens to announce the Greek victory at the Battle of Marathon would call up romantic images, it seems that the longest race run in the ancient games was about 5,000 meters. Thus the 1896 marathon was, if truth be told, probably the first ever run.

It was not an attractive race. The Frenchman Albin Lermusiaux, perhaps hoping to avenge his third-place finish in the 1,500, shot out front and at the midpoint of the race was far ahead of the pack. Passing through a small Greek village Lermusiaux was presented a victory wreath, but shortly thereafter he slowed and staggered. An alcohol rubdown initially revived him, but by this time the previous day's winner of the 800 meters, Edwin Flack, had jogged past the leader. A short distance more and Lermusiaux collapsed entirely. Flack seemed the sure winner. Four kilometers before the finish line, however, exhaustion caught up with him as well, and mistaking a bystander's attempt to steady him as an assault, the wild-eyed and wearied Australian began punching his good samaritan. It was the end of the race for Flack, who rode the remaining distance in a carriage. As the mostly Greek crowd watched for the new leader, the word was passed that a Greek was in the lead, as indeed one was—a poor and unknown shepherd named Spirdon Loues. To loud cheers Loues crossed the finish line, achieving great fame in his native country; shortly after receiving his trophy the unassuming shepherd quietly went home and never raced again.

48

Right: Bob Garrett, winner of first discus competition

BOB GARRETT

One of the youngest, strongest, most versatile and most enterprising of the first American Olympians was Robert Garrett, the twenty-year-old captain of the Princeton track-and-field team. An experienced shot putter and an all-around athlete, Garrett had heard that one of the events scheduled for the Athens games was the discus. But he had never thrown a discus, nor indeed even seen one, apart from those depicted in various ancient Greek illustrations. Still Garrett was intrigued. And challenged. Handing one of those old pictures to a college friend, he asked the fellow to fabricate a reasonable replica of a discus, which the friend did, though without much success. The thing was heavy and ungainly, and Garrett, with no training in the event and very little acquaintance with hurling techniques, had great difficulty controlling his thick metal platter. Achieving enough distance not to embarrass himself in Athens seemed an impossibility. Discouraged, he dropped the idea and concentrated on other events.

Arriving at the Olympic stadium, however, he came across the real thing lying in the grass and discovered that the official Greek discus was much lighter and more aerodynamic than his Princeton prototype. Garrett practice threw a few times, borrowed a discus, entered the competition and with his last throw beat Panagiotis Paraskevopoulos, the Greek champion, by 7½". Garrett also won the shot put with only one attempt, his first, beating his nearest Greek competitor by ¾". In addition he came in second in the high jump and might have won the long jump had Ellery Clark, who fouled on his first two jumps, not made a perfect leap on his last attempt to beat Garrett by almost a foot.

49

Hilly, uneven running track on the grounds of Racing Club of France in Paris

Paris
1900

Princeton athletes: Carroll, Chamberlain, Cregan, Perry, Jarvis (seated); Christie, Horton, Coleman (standing)

The 1900 Paris games were an Olympic event in name only—or to be more precise, not even in name only. Scheduled to coincide with the July 14 Bastille Day weekend festivities, the athletic competitions were described on the official program as simply an international track meet. In fact, many of the athletes who participated claimed to be unaware that this was a continuation of the 1896 games until they read the word "Olympic" on their medals.

By most accounts, the French organizers seemed patently uninterested in the track-and-field meet. Hardly any special provisions were made. No stadium was built. There were no royal opening ceremonies, as there had been in Athens. Competition was staged in an open field called the Pré Catalan in the Bois de Boulogne. Spectators were not seated; they simply wandered about, sometimes on the field itself, and watched.

There was a track, a 500-meter oval laid out in the grass, but it did not have a cinder path of any sort. The ground was so uneven that even the sprinters had to negotiate small hills and hollows. Discus and hammer throws sometimes crashed through the trees and bushes surrounding the grounds. There were no pits for the jumpers, and the pole vaulters were forced to jam their poles into bare earth.

As initially announced, the games were to be run on Sunday and Monday, July 15 and 16. But this schedule did not sit well with the visiting Americans, the majority of whom were students from colleges that forbade competition on the Sabbath. At first, the French officials were accommodating. Events were rescheduled to be held on Saturday and Monday. At the same time, officials warned the Americans that since Saturday was Bastille Day, few

51

Athletes and coaches of U.S. Olympic team relax in Paris

French spectators would show up. They were correct. There were hardly any spectators during the first day of competition, and the few Europeans who did appear shook their heads in amazement at the raucous American *sauvages*, marveling in particular at their colorful college uniforms.

In spite of all this, the first day went well for the Americans, who won most of their heats and the first two finals: Alvin Kraenzlein taking the 110-meter hurdles and F. W. Jarvis the 100-meter sprint. The next day was a disaster of sorts: the officials decided to reverse themselves and hold finals on Sunday. The American team protested, but there was little it could do. Votes were taken, and though Penn athletes were allowed to make their own decisions about competing, the strong Princeton, Syracuse and Michigan teams decided to stay away. Many of those favored to win their events were thus upset simply by the fact that they chose not to compete.

On Monday the track-and-field portion of the games concluded. With their entire team in action the Americans won most of their finals, losing only in the longer running races. In fact, the single French victory of the games came in the marathon, which was won by Michel Theato, a former bakery delivery boy who was accused by some, probably unjustly, of knowing the streets of Paris so well that he was on occasion able to take short cuts.

While all this confusion was taking place in the Bois de Boulogne, a number of other, sometimes remarkable events were being staged in other parts of Paris. Fencing and shooting competitions, then very popular, were held, as were soccer matches. For the first time in Olympic history, events for women were staged. Five-time Wimbledon

champion Charlotte Cooper defeated France's Helene Prevost in women's singles tennis, and Margaret Abbott won the nine-hole golf tournament, becoming the first American woman to bring home a first-place trophy.

The river Seine was one of the most popular venues during the Paris games. There was a full complement of rowing events, one of which, the pair-oared shell with coxswain, featured the youngest Olympic athlete in history, a ten-year-old boy who was placed at the last minute in a Dutch boat because it was thought his small size would ensure victory. (Whatever the reason, the Dutch did win.) Swimming events also were held in the Seine, the courses set up so that athletes swam with the current, a fact that accounted for some unusually fast times.

Two of the more curious swimming events, held for the first and last times, were underwater swimming and the obstacle race. In the first of these races, contestants were scored on distance and time underwater. The course of the obstacle race consisted of one row of boats over which the participants climbed, and then a second row of boats under which they swam. In spite of these obstacles, swimming skills seemed still to be paramount: the winner of this event was the Austrian Frederick Lane, who also finished first in the traditional 200-meter freestyle.

The Paris Olympics were probably the least ballyhooed of modern games. But there seems to be little doubt that they were fun—in fact, they sometimes seemed more like a carnival than an athletic competition. What games since have featured, for instance, the horse high and long jumps, which were won respectively by Dominique Garderes on Canela (6' ¾") and Constant Van Langhendonck aboard Extra Dry (52' 10").

53

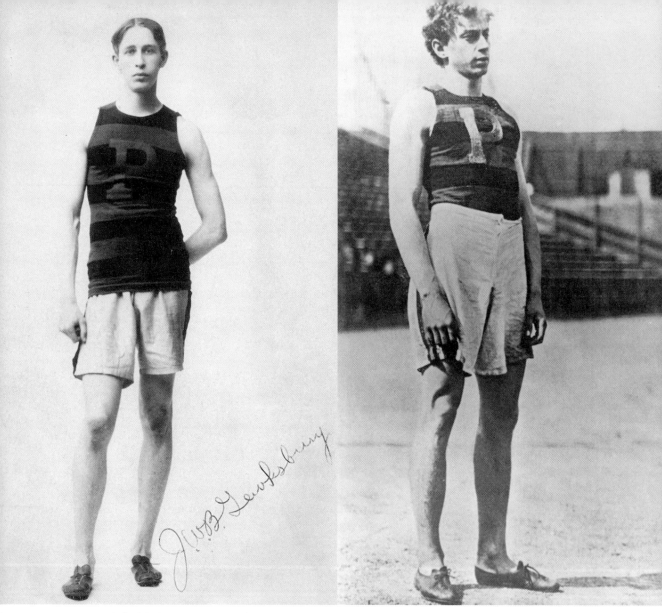

Left: John Tewksbury, winner of 200- and 400-meter hurdles. Right: A. Kraenzlein (USA), winner of 4 golds.

TEWKSBURY, BAXTER, CONNOLLY, GARRETT

The difference between victory, defeat or even the order of placement in any particular Olympic event often is not entirely dependent on pure ability. Injury, of course, has often accounted for the disappointments of some competitors, as well as the concomitant elation of others. But in other cases, the roadblocks to success have been less physical than mental. Confusions, misunderstandings, team policies, even personal and religious beliefs have constituted the crucial difference in the playing out of several Olympic events. Perhaps at no time was this more true than it was during the 1900 Paris games.

The result of the initial race of the Paris games, the 100 meters, and of many subsequent sprints was affected by a single injury. At the halfway mark the leader was Arthur Duffey of Georgetown, who most considered likely to dominate this and other short races. But all of a sudden, as Duffey remembered, "My leg gave way. I felt a peculiar twitching after going twenty yards. I then seemed to lose control of it, and suddenly it gave out, throwing me on my face. But," Duffey continued, "that is one of the fortunes of sport, and I cannot complain."

Neither, of course, could second-place finisher John Walter Tewksbury. With Duffey out of action, Tewksbury went on to finish first in both the 200 meters and the 400 meters and was able to garner a close second in the 60-meter sprint, finishing behind Alvin Kraenzlein.

Irving Baxter enjoyed similar good fortune. Bascom Johnson and Charles Dvorak were considered the best pole vaulters at the games. The two, however, were told by French officials that the finals of the event would not be

Left: John Flanagan (USA) wins first of 3 successive hammer competitions. Right: James Lightbody (left).

held on Sunday. Shortly after Johnson and Dvorak left the field, these same officials changed their minds; Baxter, who was still hanging around, entered and won the pole vault. This is not to diminish Baxter's abilities: facing a full complement of competitors he easily won the high jump, finished second in the standing high jump and placed second in both the standing long jump and the standing hop, step and jump, or standing triple jump.

The difficulties that confronted Bob Garrett and a number of other American athletes were less a shift in the winds of fortune than the result of well-considered decisions. Garrett, who had won the discus and shot put in Athens in 1896 chose, along with his fellow Princeton teammates, not to compete on Sunday. This decision benefited another thrower, Richard Sheldon, who placed third in the discus. Sheldon then went on to win the shot put, his best event; Garrett took third.

At the same time, exigencies and accidents do not fully account for the wide and sometimes surprising range of victories and placings accomplished by athletes during the Paris Olympics. All who won medals were superb athletes. Tewksbury was a talented hurdler and sprinter. Baxter won or placed in all the jumping events except the running triple jump and the running long jump. Garrett could jump as well as throw; he scored a third in the standing triple jump. Even James Connolly, one of the heroes of the 1896 games, returned in 1900 to place second in the running triple jump and third in the running long jump. Together these four American athletes brought home an impressive fourteen medals, including four golds, in thirteen different events.

55

St. Louis
1904

Harry Hillman wins 400-meter flat race, as well as 200- and 400-meter hurdles

Thirteen nations had competed in the inaugural modern Olympic Games in Athens in 1896. Four years later in Paris this total rose to twenty-two. It seemed as if the Olympic idea was catching on. But in these terms the 1904 St. Louis games were a great disappointment. Only twelve countries sent athletes, and the vast majority of competitors were Americans. One problem was the location itself, which apparently dampened the enthusiasm of those teams which had competed in 1900. (Paris presumably being a more attractive destination than St. Louis.)

None of the great collegiate track-and-field powerhouses sent athletes. Only two of those associated with the previous games showed up in St. Louis: Meyer Prinstein and Charlie Dvorak, this time under no Sabbath prohibition, won the hop, step and jump and the pole vault, respectively. In effect this transformed the games into a sort of intramural contest between the New York A.C. and the Chicago A.A., with a few independents, such as Archie Hahn, the "Milwaukee Meteor," thrown in. Hahn, a short, stocky recent graduate of the University of Michigan, monopolized the sprints. Despite running into a strong headwind, he won the 100 meters by almost 2 meters. He also easily won the 60 meters. In the 200 meters his three strongest challengers false-started and were forced to step 2 meters back. This advantage served only to lengthen Hahn's margin of victory. He won by 3 meters.

There were four other triple winners at St. Louis. American runner James Lightbody won the steeplechase and two flat races; Ray Ewry once again easily won all the standing jumps; and Harry Hillman won both hurdles races as well as the 400-meter flat race. Hillman was a twenty-two-year-old bank clerk who belonged to the New York A.C.

57

1904 ST. LOUIS 1904 Left: Ray Ewry (USA) repeats standing-event wins. Right: Fred Winders (USA), second-place dumbell finisher. ST. LOUIS 1904 ST.

An outspoken health enthusiast, he counseled fellow athletes to abstain from meat and sweets and recommended downing quantities of raw eggs. Apparently this diet was successful, for Hillman at least, as he ran away with the 200-meter hurdles and again won in the 400 meters.

The fifth athlete to win three gold medals in St. Louis has the double distinction of having swept not only all the events staged in her sport, but all those staged for her gender. In the only competitions for female athletes at the 1904 games, Lida Howell won both of the two individual archery contests and, with her teammates from the Cincinnati Archers, took first place in the team round as well.

St. Louis marked the appearance of that contingent of American throwers known as "the Whales." With the exception of the 6' 6", 235-pound Californian Ralph Rose, all were burly New York City policemen. Rose's specialty was the shot put: he won the event in both the 1904 and 1908 games and narrowly lost—to another New York cop, Patrick McDonald—in 1912. Rose also threw the discus and the hammer, placing in both several times in his Olympic career. Another Whale, John J. Flanagan, was the master of the hammer throw, gaining easy victories in all three Olympics he entered. (In 1909, at the age of forty-one, Flanagan became the oldest man to break a world track-and-field record, when he threw the hammer 184' 4".) The third-place finisher in the discus, coming in behind Flanagan and Rose, was one of the two Greek athletes who had come to St. Louis hoping to avenge their country's losses in those throwing events traditionally associated with ancient Greece. Nicolaos Georgantas entered the shot

Left: Discus champion Martin Sheridan (USA). Right: African Zulu marathoners Lentauw and Yamasani.

put, but after having his first two attempts nullified for throwing rather than putting, he dropped out. He was more successful in the discus, coming in third, even though his low trajectory style of hurling caused his discus to drop 5 feet shorter than that of Martin Sheridan, who had perfected the high trajectory, so-called American style.

The other Greek athlete at the St. Louis games was weightlifter Perikles Kakousis. Kakousis, generally acknowledged as the world champion in the super heavyweight-unlimited weightlifting event, had no credible competitor, lifting 245 lbs. to the second-place finisher, the American Oscar Osthoff's 185 lbs.

There were, of course, other non-American triumphs in 1904. British distance runners were consistently competitive, as were the Cuban fencers, particularly sixteen-year-old Ramon Fonst, who captured golds in both foil and epee. The Germans, Swiss and Austrians won or placed in the majority of the gymnastic events. One of the few Americans to do well in gymnastics was George Eyser, who improbably took first in the long horse vault despite having a wooden leg.

The final events of these sometimes chaotic Olympic Games were described by Baron de Coubertin as being possible "in no place but America." These were the Anthropology Days, a two-day track-and-field meet which featured competitions between Pygmies from Africa, Patagonians, Ainus from Japan, and Moros and Igorots from the Philippines. Many events were typical of a traditional track meet, but others, such as the mud fight, won by the Pygmies, had never appeared before, nor would they ever again appear on an Olympic program.

59

Jim Lightbody, winner of steeplechase, 800- and 1,500-meter races, accepts cup from Olympic official

JAMES LIGHTBODY

James Lightbody of the Chicago A.A. was one of the premier middle- and long-distance runners of his era. On the first day of the games Lightbody entered the steeplechase (which in 1904 was set at a distance of 2,590 meters). Among his competitors were George Bonhag, Harvey Cohn and A.L. Newton of New York as well as the Irishman John J. Daly, all of whom were listed as among those favored to win the race. Despite trailing for most of the race, Lightbody, with the help of his famous kick, passed the leaders and defeated Daly by a full second.

Three days later, Lightbody ran in the 800-meter final, a race that many observers of the time considered the greatest they had ever seen. Again the field was strong. At the start George Underwood of New York and E. W. Breitkreutz shared the lead. John Runge of Germany closed in, as did Howard Valentine of New York. But all the jostling and the stiff pace began to tell upon the leaders. About 50 meters from the finish Lightbody once again turned up the speed, and passing the leaders seemingly effortlessly crossed the finish line in first place. It was, overall, a fast race, the first three finishers all surpassing the old Olympic record by almost 5 seconds.

Two days later, Lightbody, employing almost precisely the same strategy, won the 1,500 meters. His team-mates led for most of the race. Once again, with 6 meters to go, Lightbody simply sprinted ahead and won the event. His time of 4:05.4 was not only an Olympic but also a world record. Later that afternoon, Lightbody's Chicago A.A. entered the only 4-mile team race run in Olympic history. Apparently tired, however, from the events of the week, Lightbody lost his famous kick and his team was defeated by that of the New York A.C.

Exhausted, Thomas Hicks (USA) sits in car after being named victor in controversial marathon

MARATHON

Excessive heat, dogs, green apples, egg whites, strychnine and visiting Zulu tribesmen: these are a few of the many incredible, even lunatic elements that made up the running of the 1904 Olympic marathon. The course began at the Olympic stadium and proceeded over a hilly dirt road made incredibly dusty by the large number of cars darting around the runners. The day was hot, and at the halfway point it became clear that the leaders were in trouble. Bill Garcia had swallowed so much dust that his stomach was hemorrhaging; John Lordon began vomiting; and Thomas Hicks was given a performance-enhancing mixture of egg white and strychnine in order to continue.

Back in the pack, meanwhile, Felix Carvajal, a Cuban postman, was trotting happily along, all the while eating peaches and apples and chatting with onlookers. Behind Carvajal was the Zulu, Lentauw, an Olympic concession worker who entered the race on a lark. (Lentauw eventually finished ninth, despite being chased off the course at one point by a pair of barking dogs.)

The first man to cross the finish line was Fred Lorz of the New York A.C. About to be declared winner, he laughingly admitted he had not run the entire course. Around 9 miles out Lorz had stopped and been picked up by one of the many automobiles on the road. Five miles before arriving back at the stadium the car broke down and Lorz began to jog back; thinking it a great joke he continued until he crossed the finish line. Later, after the confusion subsided, Hicks, in spite of the strychnine doping, was declared the winner. Carvajal, in baggy clothes and heavy work boots, and slightly cramped from the apples, finished a remarkable fourth.

ATHENS 1906 ATHENS 1906 The Danish women's gymnastics teams, the only women to appear in 1906, enter the stadium ATHENS 1906 ATHENS 1906

Athens
1906

The 1906 games are not, officially at least, recognized as one for the books. In 1896 Greece, viewing itself the logical homeland of the Olympics, suggested that Athens be the permanent site of the games. But it was Baron de Coubertin's hope to spread the Olympic ideal around the globe, and ignoring the request he scheduled the second revival of the games for Paris. The Greeks persisted, however, and after the somewhat disappointing turnout in St. Louis in 1904, Coubertin reluctantly agreed to allow Greece to host a series of off-year competitions, the first of which would be held in 1906.

Despite the fact that even today the results of the 1906 games are not acknowledged as Olympic records, it was in many ways the first Olympics easily recognizable as such. Of the twenty nations that sent competitors to Athens, many for the first time outfitted their athletes with national team uniforms, a change from the club and college garb worn at past games. The United States, at the urging of President Roosevelt, even organized an Olympic committee which certified those athletes who would represent the country. No longer did American athletes just wander onto the fields and compete in whatever events they wished.

As in 1896, Greece was a gracious and enthusiastic host nation. Though some complained about the ankle-deep cinders and the sharp turns of the track, the Panathenaic stadium provided a beautiful setting for the games. And again King George of Greece was in constant attendance, as were his sons Nicholas, George, Andrew and Constantine, the latter of whom was president of the Greek Olympic Committee.

Women's singles and men's doubles competition on Athens Olympic tennis court

The 1906 Olympics were opened with the kind of pomp and fanfare so much lacking during the past two games. As part of the opening ceremonies an exhibition of gymnastic exercises was performed by "short-skirted and neat-legged" Danish girls. This was followed by a demonstration of geriatric fitness by the fifty-six-year-old British athlete J. E. Fowler-Dixon, who as a sign of his prowess walked the 1,500-meter track in under 9 minutes, caught his breath for a few minutes and then ran the same distance in under 6 minutes.

As there had been in the past, there were competitive events held in and out of the stadium: shooting, cycling, fencing, swimming, gymnastics, weightlifting. For the most part the winners of these events were Europeans. (The French, Italians and Dutch did well in fencing; the British in cycling and the Norwegians and French in gymnastics.) Swimming was once again held in the open waters of the bay, where Charlie Daniels of the United States and Henry Taylor of Great Britain won the first of the several medals each would collect in the Olympics.

There were certain definite but puzzling changes. For some reason the Greeks decided to omit some of the events usually held. In 1906, for instance, there were no 60- or 200-meter sprints, no 200- or 400-meter hurdles and no 2,500-meter steeplechase. This meant that some past medalists, such as sprinter Archie Hahn and hurdler Harry Hillman, were limited as to the number of their possible victories.

Hahn, who was widely considered the fastest man in the world, may have had a strategic advantage over his opponents. There were four Americans in the final: Hahn, Fay Moulton, W. D. Eaton and Lawson Robertson. Talking

Start of 100 meters final, won by American Archie Hahn (second from right)

among themselves before the race, the Americans observed that the starter used exactly the same cadence each time he sent the runners on their way. What the runners would do, all agreed, was take off during the last syllable of that pentultimate command. But, Robertson has said, "Hahn was smarter than all of us. He started as soon as the Greek spoke his first syllable and the rest of us were left in the dust."

Though the usual full-scale track meet was significantly abbreviated, two new events were added to the program. One of these, the pentathlon, was won by the Swedish athlete Hjalmar Mellander, who outscored his opponents in the standing long jump, Greek-style discus, 192-meter race, javelin and Greco-Roman wrestling. (These were the events of the ancient Greek penthalon, not those of the modern penthalon, which was first held in 1912.) The other new event, the javelin throw, was won by another Swede, the Stockholm policeman Eric Lemming.

The 1906 games marked the emergence of yet another Northern European nation, Finland, as a world power in Olympic athletics. Though he placed third in the freestyle discus, Verner Jarvinen, the first Finn to compete in the Olympics, won the Greek-style discus, an event that required the thrower to pose on a forward sloping pedestal and release the discus from a standing position. (Second in that event was Nicolaos Georgantas, who after his disappointments in St. Louis delighted the Greek home country crowd by easily winning the 14.08-pound stone throw.)

Another 1906 medalist had also been frustrated in St. Louis. The American distance runner George Bonhag came to Athens intent upon gaining a first-place finish. But after coming in fourth in his specialty, the 5-mile run,

E. B. Archibald (CAN) clears the pole

Bonhag decided to enter the 1,500-meter walk, an event in which he had never previously competed.

Walking events, due to their stringent rules (competitors must always keep one foot touching the ground— "lifting" results in immediate ejection—and must straighten the leg with each step), were notoriously controversial, and this particular race was no exception.

At first it seemed that the favorite in this event, Richard Wilkinson of Great Britain, would breeze to victory, until one of the judges, Prince George, disqualified him for improper technique. (Wilkinson pretended not to understand but finally quit when George commanded, in English, "Leave! You have finished.") Disqualification followed disqualification, and suddenly Bonhag found himself in the lead, heel and toeing across the finish line, as one observer noted, "shaking with laughter."

Prince George, always an active organizer, also figured in the dramatic finish of the marathon. After Spiridon Loues's victory in 1896, the Greek crowd had great hopes that another countryman would win what it thought of as Greece's race. But William Sherring of Canada had come to Greece a month in advance of the games in order to practice and was well ahead of the pack as he entered the stadium. Despite the disappointment of the crowd, which shouted "Xenos" (foreigner), as Sherring appeared, Prince George jogged the last lap with the winner and led him to the royal box to be congratulated by the queen. Political difficulties prevented the staging of a 1910 off-year Olympics, and soon the idea, never popular with Coubertin anyway, just faded away.

Upset-winner Paul Pilgrim (USA) followed by Halswelle (GBR) and Barker (AUS) in 400 meters final

PAUL PILGRIM

By all odds Paul Pilgrim should not have been a double winner at the 1906 games. In fact, he should not have competed in Athens at all. The U.S. Olympic organizing committee had chosen a strong middle-distance team. Harry Hillman, who had won the 400 meters in St. Louis, and Jim Lightbody, the 1904 800-meters champion, were on the squad, as were Fay Moulton and Charley Bacon, both fine runners. At the last moment, however, James Sullivan, the head of the committee, told team manager Matt Halpin that fund-raising had been so successful that one extra man could be added to the team. Halpin chose Pilgrim, a talented but inexperienced young man whom he was coaching at the New York A.C.

At Athens Pilgrim ran well enough to qualify for the finals in the 400. But he had stiff competition: not only Hillman but also Lieutenant Wyndham Halswelle of Great Britain and the Australian Nigel Barker. Unfortunately for Hillman, however, his leg had been injured in a shipboard accident on the way to Greece, and about halfway through he pulled up and was for all intents and purposes out of the race. At this point it was a two-man race, Halswelle and Barker pulling ahead. A few yards from the finish, however, Pilgrim took off and beat the two leaders by a meter.

The next day was the 800-meter race and Lightbody, usually noted for his great finishing kick, uncharacteristically took the lead. But 50 meters from the finish line, Pilgrim did it again. He caught up with the famed kicker and amazingly enough outsprinted him, winning his second first-place in two days. It might be unfair to characterize Pilgrim as a one-Olympic wonder, but it is true that he had never won a major race before nor would he again.

Left: All-around athlete Martin Sheridan throws hammer

MARTIN SHERIDAN

There are some athletes so gifted that their performances have a playful, spirited, almost effortless feeling to them. It is not just an excess of competitive drive, though that is plainly apparent. It is more a matter of a seemingly magical ability to enjoy the life of their sport. They seem above all to be having fun.

The American Olympian Martin Sheridan is one of these rare athletes. Sheridan first appeared in Olympic competition in St. Louis in 1904. Though he was included as a member of that group of throwers dubbed "the Whales," Sheridan, a New York City policeman, was clearly not as beefy as either the shot putter Ralph Rose or the hammer specialist John Flanagan. Tall and muscular, he could have passed for a runner or a jumper or indeed any of the other track-and-field competitors.

In fact, one wonders how Sheridan might have fared as a decathlete. (The only decathlon held before the 1912 introduction of that event into the Olympic program was staged in St. Louis, but that competition, with all ten components held in a single day, appears to have been considered somewhat of a lark and Sheridan apparently stuck to his usual events.)

At St. Louis, Sheridan won his speciality, the discus, and placed fourth in the shot put. But as in all the games in which he competed, Sheridan somehow always managed to be in the thick of other sorts of Olympic action. Along with his fellow Whales, Sheridan adopted the Cuban marathoner Felix Carvajal, who after being swindled of his money in a New Orleans craps game, arrived in St. Louis penniless and hungry. Sheridan fed Carvajal, and shortly

68

Center: John Flanagan, three-time hammer gold medalist. Right: Ralph Rose, double gold medalist in shot put.

before the start of the marathon grabbed a pair of shears and tailored the Cuban postman's heavy street clothes into a running uniform of sorts. With this help Carvajal finished in fourth place.

Two years later in Athens, despite a shipboard accident, Sheridan entered a total of six events. He again won the discus, as well as the shot put, and placed second in the 14-pound stone throw and fourth in the Greek-style discus. Sheridan also competed, for what appears to have been the sheer sport of it, in the standing high jump and the standing long jump. (In both events, he came in second behind his friend Ray Ewry.) Finally, he also tried his hand at a new event, the pentathlon, and was doing extremely well when his injured knee finally gave out on him.

In 1908, Sheridan competed in his third and last Olympics, winning both discus events and coming in third in the standing high jump. But again it was not only on the athletic field that Sheridan distinguished himself. Just before the opening of the London games American athletes noticed that their flag was missing from among those flying over the stadium. British officials apologized, saying that it was an oversight, but Sheridan had his revenge. As he entered the stadium, he refused, as had been the custom, to dip the flag he was carrying in front of the British king. "This flag," he later announced, "dips to no earthly king."

Though Sheridan continued to be active in the New York A.C., 1908 was the last year he competed in the Olympics. Perhaps he took to heart the advice he gave to Ewry after the London competition. "Ray," Sheridan said, "you're getting to be an old man. You ought to quit."

LONDON 1908 LONDON 1908 First-time partners Schilles and Auffray of France win 2,000-meter tandem race   LONDON 1908 LONDON 1908 LOND

London
1908

British athletes march into Shepherd's Bush stadium

It is tempting to call the 1908 London games the last of the first generation of Olympic competitions: colorful, contentious, often governed by a shifting set of arbitrary rules and rulings. Like all the previous Olympics it was organized, administered and officiated by the host country, and this fact caused continual controversy.

Americans complained about the track-and-field officiating, which they considered an expression of anti-American sentiment. But the Americans weren't the only ones troubled by what was perceived as British bias. Italians protested the disqualification of marathoner Dorando Pietri. The Canadians and the French considered rulings made during many of the cycling events outrageous. And the Swedes withdrew entirely from the Greco-Roman wrestling following what they thought were plainly unfair decisions made by British referees.

In spite of all of this, it may be more accurate to term the London games transitional. All the controversy (and hardly a day went by without some sort of squabbling) convinced Olympic organizers that in the future judging should be done by internationally recognized experts who would presumably not be saddled with the chauvinism with which the British were charged. All told, however, blame for the many controversies that erupted during the London games was, as American track-and-field athlete Lawson Robertson later said, "equally distributed among competing nations." It was also evident, he added, that "England was not as charitably inclined toward the American champions as she might have been, and it is equally true that the victorious Americans were not as modest as they should have been."

71

Protesting Sunday competition, 110-meter gold medalist Smithson (USA) hurdles with Bible

Certainly in many ways the British athletic establishment did a remarkable job of preparation. A huge and well-designed stadium was constructed at Shepherd's Bush in the west of London. Built to accommodate 68,000 spectators, it contained a cinder track measuring three laps to the mile, a running surface far superior to those of other past venues. Inside the track was a swimming pool, and circling it was a banked cycling track.

The marathon, which in the past had been anywhere between 20 and 40 miles in length, was laid out at 26 miles, 385 yards, this being the exact distance between the starting line on the grounds of Windsor Castle and the finish line, which was placed directly in front of the royal box in the Shepherd's Bush stadium. From 1908 on, this distance, arbitrarily set so that the queen would have a good view of the finish line, has been generally recognized as the standard length of the race.

The games' ceremonies began on July 17, as did almost immediately the notorious English rain. It continued to rain throughout the games, sometimes in torrents, sometimes just enough to make the competitors miserable. Given these conditions it was often difficult for athletes to match their best times and distances. The American throwers, who competed on the earliest and wettest days of the games, were continually slipping and sliding and wallowing about. (Despite their gripes they still dominated their events.)

Another event, the outcome of which should have not been affected by conditions, was protested for a different reason. In the final of the tug-of-war, the American team charged that members of the opposing team, made

Freestyle match watched over by Olympic official at White City wrestling venue

up of Liverpool "Bobbies," were wearing "monstrous boots." Not so, countered British officials. These boots were everyday footwear, the shoes these men normally wore while walking their beats on the Liverpool streets.

Fittingly the 1908 Olympics, perhaps the most disputatious of the early games, concluded with what turned out to be the least competitive race in Olympic history. In the final of the 400-meter run four runners, three from the United States and one, the favorite, Lieutenant Wyndham Halswelle, from London, had won their heats and stood at the starting line. British officials, worried that the Americans would gang up on Halswelle, stationed spotters every 20 meters on the track, instructing them to be on the lookout for lane violations. William Robbins, one of the Americans, took an early lead but at the halfway point was passed by Halswelle and another of the Americans, John Carpenter. Halswelle attempted to pass but Carpenter ran wide, blocking the British runner. The official nearest the action called a foul and another ran across the track and cut the worsted string at the finish line. A third official actually yanked the fourth American, John Taylor, off the track. After much arguing between British and Americans, Carpenter was disqualified and the race was ordered to be rerun two days later. American officials continued to maintain that there had been no foul. As Carpenter later described the race, "Halswelle had lots of room to pass me on either side. We just raced him off his feet. He couldn't stand the pace."

Two days later the 400 final was again run, but this time without any of the Americans, who as a protest refused to race. This left Halswelle to run alone, which he did, winning the gold medal with a time of 50.0 seconds.

Top: Marathoners at start by Windsor Castle. Bottom: Pietri (ITA) approaches stadium.

MARATHON

The running of the marathon on the next-to-the-last day of track-and-field competition began much as expected, with British runners T. Jack, Fred Lord and Jack Price in the lead. Perhaps buoyed by the cheers of the thousands of English fans lining the route of the race, the three picked up the pace—a mistake, as it turned out. By the 5-mile mark Jack had faltered; at 10 miles Lord dropped back; and after 14 miles the two leaders were Charles Hefferon, a South African, and Dorando Pietri, the diminutive Italian.

For the next few miles, Hefferon held the lead, sometimes running 3 or 4 minutes ahead of Pietri. Two miles from the stadium, however, the excited leader stopped to accept a celebratory glass of champagne from a spectator. Within minutes after returning to the race the alcohol began to work on his exhausted body; his stomach cramped and he experienced dizzy spells. Hefferon painfully continued to run, but he was easily passed by Pietri, who, climbing the steep hill leading to Wormwood Prison, took the lead with only 2 miles to go.

None of this was known by those waiting in the stadium, who, having heard that the South African was well in the lead, were amazed to see Pietri, a little man in a baggy shirt and short red pants, enter and begin the final jog to the finish line. Spectators, as well as race officials, were even more surprised when the obviously tired Pietri turned the wrong way and stumbled from the finish line. One of the trackside officials ran to Pietri and turned him in the right direction, but a few yards later Pietri collapsed.

As someone in the stadium described him, "The man was practically delirious. He staggered along the cinder

74

Disoriented, Pietri is guided across finish line

path like a man in a dream, his gait being neither a walk nor a run but simply a floundering with arms shaking and legs tottering." Pietri collapsed again and again was helped to his feet. Indeed, five times he fell, and he was able to cross the finish line only with the support of track officials. After a final slump and spill, he was carried off unconscious on a stretcher by medical personnel who worried that he was near death.

Fans were further surprised to see not Hefferon but the American Johnny Hayes, a twenty-year-old department store clerk, enter the stadium and jog across the finish line in second place. Hayes was also a small man, 5' 5" tall and weighing only 127 pounds, but he had run a well-considered race. At 20 miles, with the leaders nowhere in sight, he stepped up his pace. "You're going too fast," his running mate Mike Ryan yelled. "We've got to move now, stick with me," Hayes replied.

Hayes's strategy worked. Just before reaching the stadium he passed the cramped and tired Hefferon and finished the race a minute after Pietri had been helped across the finish line. American officials immediately lodged a protest. Pietri had been aided, a clear violation of the rules. Despite the sympathy of the crowd for Pietri, the referees had no choice but to agree. Hayes was declared the winner and was carried off on a makeshift platform. The next day Pietri protested that he could have completed the race on his own, a claim that no one in the stadium that afternoon believed. Sympathy for Pietri was so overwhelming, however, that he instantly became a worldwide sensation. Furthermore, his courageous efforts sparked a surge of interest in the marathon which continues to this day.

Left: Ewry (USA), winner of standing long jump. Right: Ewry clears 6' in standing high jump final.

RAY EWRY

It is not clear why the standing jump events were included in Olympic competition nor why, after four sets of games, they were discontinued. What is certain is that the three chief standing jump events (standing high jump, standing long jump and standing hop, step and jump, or triple jump) were the personal province of a single athlete, the long-legged, lanky, former polio victim Ray Ewry, a man whose ability to spring from rest into long airborne vertical and horizontal leaps even now is hard to believe.

As the *New York Mail and Express* described the most astonishing of Ewry's feats, the standing high jump, "Ewry's performance is marvelous. A man who can stand still before a bar five feet five inches high and lift himself over it must not only have wonderful spring, but also the ability to handle his legs very rapidly. The standing high jump is made by the athlete standing sideways to the bar. When the spring is made, the leg near the stick is put over first, and it begins descending before the trailing leg is well up. The dropping of the forward leg over the bar after clearing it counterbalances the raising of the trailing leg. It is essentially a motion which only can be acquired with much practice and differs very much from the standing broad jump, the movements of which are so simple that anyone can go through them. Ewry's record is apt to stand a long time." It is interesting to compare Ewry's gold medal–winning heights and distances with those in running versions of the same events. In looking at the chart opposite, note that the standing triple jump was discontinued as an Olympic event after 1904; otherwise Ewry would quite possibly—and remarkably—have won all three standing jumps four games in a row.

76

Following pages: British police tug-of-war. National archery, won by "Queenie" Newhall (GBR).

**EWRY'S GOLD-MEDAL RESULTS VERSUS THE GOLD-MEDAL RESULTS
IN RUNNING VERSION OF SAME EVENTS**

Ewry's Standing Triple Jump Distances		Running Triple Jump Winning Distances
34' 8½"	-1900-	47' 5 ¾"
37' 7¼"	-1904-	47' 1"

Ewry's Standing High Jump Heights		Running High Jump Winning Heights		Ewry's Standing Long Jump Distances		Running Long Jump Winning Distances
5' 5"	-1900-	6' 2¾"		6' 1¼"	-1900-	26' 6¾"
5' 3"	-1904-	5' 11"		11' 4⅞"	-1904-	24' 1"
5' 1¼"	-1906-	5' 10"		10' 10"	-1906-	23' 7½"
5' 2"	-1908-	6' 3"		10' 11¼"	-1908-	24' 6½"

Stockholm 1912

Norwegian gymnastics team, winner of the free exercise and apparatus competition

By the time it was announced that Stockholm would be the site of the 1912 Olympic Games, the world had begun to take the games very seriously. This was particularly true of Northern Europe. And these countries had begun to achieve successes seemingly out of proportion to their relatively small sizes. In 1912, for instance, more than a third of the gold medals awarded in track-and-field were won by athletes from Sweden, Finland and Norway.

The Stockholm games were also the best organized to date. A beautiful new stadium with seating for 30,000 spectators was constructed. Swimming events were held in a nearby pool. Officials were well trained. Trials and heats were scheduled to run smoothly. The nearly 2,500 athletes from twenty-eight nations were all well housed and their needs graciously accommodated. For the first time in Olympic history electric timing, calibrated to 1/10 of a second, and photo-finish systems were installed on the track. And as if to seemingly justify its existence and utility, timing equipment was needed to break apparent dead heat ties for second place in two races.

In the 800 meters Mel Sheppard, who had won the event in London four years earlier, was expected to be challenged by the great German runner Hanns Braun. But the U.S. team had a strategy. Sheppard's teammate, nineteen-year-old Ted Meredith, was to set a fast pace in hopes of burning out Braun and enabling Sheppard to sprint past the German in the final meters of the race. Unaccountably Sheppard took an initial lead. Meredith, perhaps confused, kept up the pace, with Braun at his heels. Pushed by Braun, Meredith sped up and before he knew it passed Sheppard, winning the race by half a meter. By this time Braun had dropped well back; the photographic equipment

83

Takedown in Greco-Roman match, the only type of wrestling held in 1912

was needed to declare Sheppard the second-place winner—inches ahead of another American, Ira Davenport.

Three days later the newly installed photo equipment was again used to sort out second and third places in the highly competitive 1,500-meter race. On the last lap the American Abel Kiviat took the lead, with his teammates John Paul Jones and Norman Taber close behind. As the three neared the finish line the Englishman Arnold Jackson began to gain on the leaders and managed at the last second to pass Kiviat and take the race. To most eyes it appeared that Kiviat and Taber had crossed the finish line absolutely together. When the finish-line photograph was developed it showed Kiviat in the lead by less than 2", and he was awarded second place.

Split-second intervals were definitely not needed to measure victory in two other remarkable contests. In Greco-Roman wrestling competitors are not allowed to grab the legs of their opponents, nor indeed to use the legs aggressively. For this reason, Greco-Roman wrestlers spend considerable time locked in what looks like a bear-hug dance. In two of the Greco-Roman matches in 1912 this struggle went on seemingly ad infinitum. In what has turned out to be the longest match in Olympic history, Alfred Asikainen of Sweden and the Estonian Martin Klein wrestled on and on in their middleweight semifinal, stopping every half-hour for a drink of water, until 11 hours after the match began, Klein finally pinned his opponent. Klein, however, was so exhausted by his day in the hot sun that he withdrew from the final, giving Claes Johanson of Sweden the victory by default. The two wrestlers in the light heavyweight class almost matched this record. Though the Swedish wrestler Anders Ahlgren had breezed through his

84

Swedish gold medalists in the 30-meter team rapid-fire pistol competition

early matches, in the final he and Ivar Böhling of Finland fought for hours with no sign of one overpowering the other. The referee, perhaps mindful of what had happened the previous day, stopped the wrestlers after 9 hours. Since there had been no clear victory Ahlgren and Böhling were declared tied for second place.

Many of the other events taking place in and around the Stockholm stadium were equally exciting. The American sprinter Ralph Craig swept both the 100- and 200-meter races. The marathon was won by the South African Kenneth McArthur after his teammate Christian Gitsham stopped for a drink 2 miles from the stadium. (Gitsham apparently thought that McArthur would politely stop and wait for him.) And the shot put was won by the newest member of the Whales, the 350-pound New York City policeman Patrick "Babe" McDonald, who for years was known as the huge cop who directed traffic at the Times Square corner of 43rd Street and Broadway.

There were also two standouts in the swimming competitions. The Hawaiian-born Duke Kahanamoku, competing in his first games, was so far ahead in the 100-meter freestyle that at the halfway mark he looked over his shoulder and decided to slow up. He still won easily. And in women's swimming, held for the first time in 1912, the remarkable Australian Fanny Durack won the 100 meters, seemingly as effortlessly as Kahanamoku. Indeed, had there been more freestyle events staged, Durak might have won them all, as she had at one time or other held the world's record in every distance from 50 yards to a mile. (There was a 4 X 100 freestyle relay race held in 1912, but unaccountably, Australians were not among the top finishers.)

85

Decathlon champion Jim Thorpe (USA) competes in discus (left) and 1,500 meters (right)

JIM THORPE

Was Jim Thorpe the greatest all-around athlete of the first half of the twentieth century, as he was voted by a 1950 Associated Press poll? Certainly it seems so. Though the only really accurate way to measure one athlete against another is to put them on the field in direct competition with each other, on paper Thorpe's varied accomplishments are nothing short of astonishing.

In 1912, playing football for small Carlisle College, Thorpe almost single-handedly defeated the football power Army. In that game he scored two touchdowns, passed for another, and kicked three field goals and three extra points. When one of these touchdowns, a 90-yard kick return, was nullified by a penalty, Thorpe trotted back to his end of the field, caught the new kick and returned it once again for a touchdown, this time running 95 yards.

That same year he practically defeated an entire collegiate track-and-field team by himself. The story is told that in May 1912 Carlisle showed up for a meet with Lafayette College with just two people on its roster, Thorpe and a student manager. This tale, of course, like many other anecdotes about Thorpe, is plainly apocryphal. Actually there were seven athletes, including Thorpe, on the Carlisle team. But these seven did defeat Lafayette 71–41, with Thorpe scoring victories in six events—the high jump, the broad jump, shot put, discus, 120-yard high hurdles and 220-yard low hurdles.

All who saw Thorpe compete were amazed not only by his astonishing athletic abilities, but also by the ease with which he seemed to perform. Abel Kiviat, the silver medalist in the 1,500, remembered being in a hotel with a

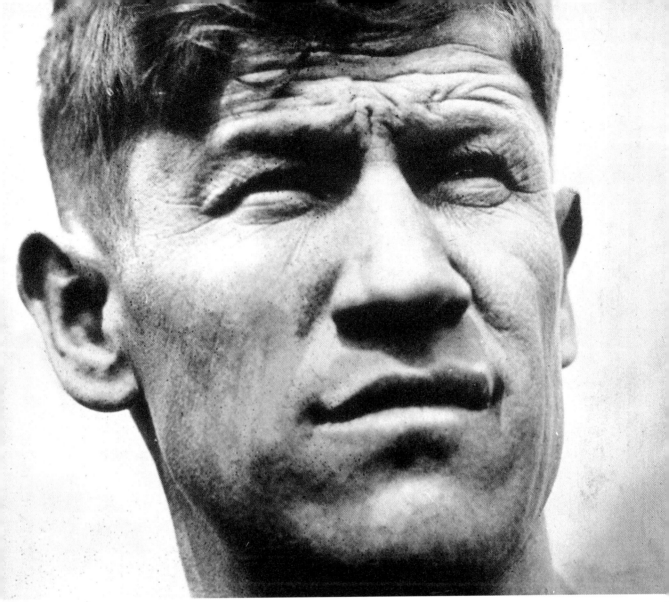

Thorpe was called the "greatest athlete in the world" by Swedish King Gustav V

group of Olympic athletes and discovering "a chandelier that must have been at least 10 feet off the floor. We all put a dollar in a pot to see if anybody could touch it. Everybody tried it. Alma Richards of Brigham Young, who won the high jump at six feet, four inches, tried, but he couldn't. But Jim Thorpe did, and he was about four inches shorter than Richards." Thorpe also played professional football and baseball for many years.

After being chosen for the American Olympic squad and arriving in Stockholm, Thorpe did not join his teammates on the practice field, preferring to spend his time napping. When it was time to compete he simply got up and did what he had to do, better, it turned out, and more often than any other athlete at the 1912 games. Thorpe competed in four events: the pentathlon, the decathlon, the high jump, and the long jump, winning the first two and placing fourth and seventh respectively in the last two. But even these numbers do not accurately reflect Thorpe's amazing feats at Stockholm. All in all, counting the five in the pentathlon and the ten in the decathlon, he competed in seventeen finals, a record that surely will never be broken.

In January 1913 Thorpe was, by virtue of some minor league baseball he had played previously, declared a professional, stripped of his medals and barred from competing in future Olympic games. How would this great athlete match up with those who followed? Given all the variables (training, track conditions and so forth) this is probably an impossible question to answer. But those who competed against him in 1912 had no doubt about his abilities. When his gold medals were offered to the second-place finishers in the decathlon and pentathlon both refused the honor.

Hannes Kolehmainen (FIN; left) and Jean Bouin (FRA)

HANNES KOLEHMAINEN

There were three long-distance runners in the Kolehmainen family: Wille, a professional, and his two younger brothers Tatu and Hannes. Unable to compete in the Olympics due to his professional status, Wille left Finland in 1910 and, though he spoke almost no English, traveled about North America in order to glean what training and strategic information he could from American and Canadian coaches and athletes.

Returning to Finland he began to coach his brothers, both of whom were set to compete in the 1912 games. Tatu, a marathoner, was leading his race through the halfway point, when he was passed by the eventual winner, Ken McArthur of South Africa. But it was twenty-two-year-old Hannes who was the great star of the long-distance events. Hannes easily won his first race of the games, coming in well ahead of the pack in the 10,000 meters. Two days later, in the 5,000 meters, he won again, this time not as easily. Early in the race Hannes and the great French star Jean Bouin distanced themselves from the rest of the field, with Bouin in front and Hannes at his shoulder. For the rest of the race the two jockeyed for position, but every time Hannes tried to pass, Bouin blocked him. Finally, just meters from the finish line, Bouin stumbled and the Finn crossed the finish line in the lead.

Hannes also ran in the 3,000-meter team race; despite his setting a world record in the event, his team was eliminated due to the slower combined times of his Finnish teammates. But Kolehmainen was not done. Two days later he entered, and handily won, the 12,000-meter team cross-country race. All in all Hannes ran, and won, 30,000 meters' worth of races at Stockholm.

Above: Sheppard (USA; left) in 1908. Following pages: U.S. athletes play exhibition baseball in 1912

THE FLYING FINNS
The Finnish dynasty in long-distance races was ushered in by Kolehmainen in 1912.

5,000m

1912	H. Kolehmainen	1st
1920	P. Nurmi	2nd
1924	P. Nurmi	1st
	V. Ritola	2nd
1928	V. Ritola	1st
	P. Nurmi	2nd
1932	L. Lehtinen	1st
	L. Virtanen	3rd
1936	G. Hockert	1st
	L. Lehtinen	2nd

Marathon

1920	H. Kolehmainen	1st
1924	A. Stenroos	1st
1928	M. Marttelin	3rd
1932	A. Toivonen	3rd

3,000m Steeplechase

1924	V. Ritola	1st
1928	T. Loukola	1st
1932	V. Iso-Hollo	1st
1936	V. Iso-Hollo	1st

10,000m

1912	H. Kolehmainen	1st
	A. Stenroos	3rd
1920	P. Nurmi	1st
1924	V. Ritola	1st
	E. Berg	3rd
1928	P. Nurmi	1st
	V. Ritola	2nd
1932	V. Iso-Hollo	2nd
	L. Virtanen	3rd
1936	I. Salminen	1st
	A. Askola	2nd

Cross-Country

1912	H. Kolehmainen	1st
1920	P. Nurmi	1st
1924	P. Nurmi	1st

Cross-Country Team

1912	Finland	2nd
1920	Finland	1st
1924	Finland	1st

e Olympiade - Anvers 1920.
filé des Athlètes (États Unis d'Amérique.)

Antwerp 1920

U.S. General John Pershing congratulates American athlete

It wouldn't be completely wrong to describe the 1920 Antwerp Olympics as one of the gloomier games ever held. World War I had ended just a year earlier, and the residents of Belgium, along with most other Europeans, had not as yet recovered from the depredations of the war. The Belgians did build a fine, new stadium, but few local residents could afford even the ten cents admission charge, and on most days fewer than a third of the seats were filled.

In addition the athletes often struggled with difficult physical conditions. Continual rain softened and muddied the track. And it was cold, particularly for the swimmers and divers. American Aileen Riggin, the fourteen-year-old springboard diving champion, remembered the swimming venue: "It was just a ditch. The water was entirely black. It was dark, dark black. The water was the coldest we had ever encountered. It was simply freezing. The swimmers bravely tried to do their laps, but some of the girls were carried out almost unconscious."

In most ways, however, the games were successful and exciting. The 2,500 athletes in attendance marched into the stadium on opening day and together, for the first time, took the Olympic oath. Over the field the five-ringed Olympic flag flew, symbolizing the interlocking of the five great landmasses.

There was also a busy schedule of events taking place around the city. The cycling road race was run through the streets of Antwerp. The course was on occasion bisected by railway crossings, at which officials were stationed to keep track of any time cyclists were forced to sit and wait for trains to pass. The presumed winner of the race

Triple gold-medalist Ugo Frigero of Italy well in the lead in the 10,000-meter walk

was Henry Kaltenbrun of South Africa, but after officials discovered that the arrival of Swedish cyclist Harry Stenqvist at the finish line had been delayed for four minutes by a train, he was awarded the gold.

Boxing, after being expunged by Swedish officials as being barbaric, returned to the Olympic program. There were soccer and shooting matches. And in fencing the 1912 individual foil champion Nedo Nadi won five gold medals: individuals in foil and sabre and, as leader of the Italian squad, team victories in foil, epee and sabre.

Multiple victories in track-and-field were of a different sort. In the past the United States had dominated these events. But in Antwerp Finnish athletes equaled the Americans in the number of their victories. Hannes Kolehmainen, one of the stars of the Stockholm games, won the marathon. His young teammate Paavo Nurmi narrowly lost his first race, the 5,000 meters, but went on to win both the 10,000-meter flat run and the 10,000-meter cross-country race. Finnish throwers dethroned the American Whales in most events. Jonni Myyra won the first of his two gold medals in the javelin throw. Ville Porhola soundly beat defending champion "Babe" McDonald in the shot put, and no American came close to Elmer Niklander's winning discus throw. Finally Vilho Tuulos won the triple jump, giving Finland its eighth medal of the games.

These Finnish victories did little to cheer up the already unhappy Americans. The track-and-field team had been sent to Belgium aboard an old Army transport, a funeral ship in fact, which had few amenities. Arriving in Antwerp after a long and uncomfortable voyage, the athletes discovered their quarters to be in an old, drafty schoolhouse

American Olympian about to release hammer

outfitted with cots. Worse, they had a 10 P.M. curfew. The American team staged an insurrection of sorts, threatening to refuse to compete when triple jumper Dan Ahearn was suspended after returning late. American officials took the threat seriously; Ahearn was reinstated and the athletes agreed to compete.

Once attention was returned to the competitive fields, the American trip proved not to be a complete failure. Babe McDonald, at forty-two the oldest person to win an Olympic field event, took first in the 56-pound weight throw. Pat Ryan won the hammer throw, the fifth consecutive time an American had done so. And Dick Landon won the high jump by leaping 6' 4⅕". (After Landon's victory the 6' 4" tall King Albert of Belgium went up to him, exclaiming, "You jumped higher than my head.")

The Canadian team scored one major victory when Earl Thomson won the 110-meter high hurdles, setting a new world record. Thomson, who attended college in the United States and who had many friends on the American team, was significantly aided in the final by Cornell trainer Jack Moakley, who bound up Thomson's injured leg by means of his newly developed "basket weave" taping technique.

The most good-natured and entertaining victor in Antwerp was the world-champion walker Ugo Frigero of Italy. Frigero, a lover of music, gave the stadium band a list of selections he would like played and sometimes waved his arms like a band leader as he passed the musicians. He easily won both of his races, the 3,000- and the 10,000-meter walks, though once during the 3,000 he slowed long enough to yell to the band that their tempo was off.

Paavo Nurmi defeats Wilhelm Scharer of Switzerland in the 1924 1,500 meters

PAAVO NURMI

Paavo Nurmi, almost certainly the greatest Olympic long-distance runner, narrowly lost in his first attempt at Olympic gold. Coming to compete in Antwerp at the age of twenty-three, Nurmi was already a semi-mythological figure. As a child, it was said, he enjoyed chasing and catching up with the local milk train. It was also reported that while in the army he took part in a 20-kilometer march, during which he decided to run, not walk, all the while carrying a rifle, ammunition and eleven pounds of sand in his knapsack.

Nurmi's great opponent in Antwerp was the Frenchman Joseph Guillemot, who despite being gassed during World War I still had enough lung power to win almost every race he entered. In the first of their three matches, the 5,000 meters, Nurmi led for most of the race, but in the final lap Guillemot burst past him and won by almost 10 meters.

Several days later, in the 10,000-meter race, the events of the previous race were exactly reversed. Guillemot set the pace, with Nurmi following, and at about the same distance the Finnish runner kicked past the Frenchman to win comfortably.

The last time the two met was in the cross-country race. Again the Frenchman and the Finn dueled for the lead, but unfortunately toward the end of the race Guillemot stepped in a hole and sprained his ankle, enabling Nurmi to coast to an easy victory. This competition with Guillemot proved to be a precursor to one of the most heated rivalries in running.

Right: "Flying Finn" Paavo Nurmi, "created to annihilate time," relaxes in infield

THE DOMINANT DISTANCE RUNNERS OF THE OLYMPICS

PAAVO NURMI (FIN)		EMIL ZÁTOPEK (CZE)		LASSE VIREN (FIN)	
1920		**1948**		**1972**	
5,000m	2nd	5,000m	2nd	5,000m	1st/OR
10,000m	1st	10,000m	1st/OR	10,000m	1st/WR
Cross Country	1st				
		1952		**1976**	
1924		5,000m	1st/OR	5,000m	1st
5,000m	1st/OR	10,000m	1st/OR	10,000m	1st
Cross Country	1st	Marathon	1st/OR	Marathon	5th
1,500m	1st/OR				
3,000m Team	1st				
1928				OR = Olympic Record	
5,000m	2nd			WR = World Record	
10,000m	1st/OR				

American sprinter Charley Paddock's 6' airborne finish-line leap

CHARLEY PADDOCK

The Olympic sprint field has traditionally been one of the most competitive of the games. This was perhaps never more true than during the three sets of games held in the 1920s. The Americans, as usual, sent strong sprint teams, which included Frank Wycoff, Loren Murchison, Jackson Scholz and Bob McAllister, "The Flying Cop" from New York City. British runners such as Jack London, Eric Liddell, Harold Abrahams and Harry Edwards were also consistently in the running, as were Arthur Porritt of New Zealand, Georg Lammers of Germany and 1928 100 meters upset winner Percy Williams of Canada.

But no sprinter was more popular and more closely associated with the Olympic sprints during this period than the American Charley Paddock, who was often called "The World's Fastest Human." Indeed, Paddock was extremely fast. Prior to the Antwerp games he had run the 100 meters in 10.8 seconds and the 200 meters in 21.6 seconds—times which would have been fast enough to win Olympic titles. But along with his rare speed, it was Paddock's style that so fascinated many observers. As one wrote:

> When Charley's foot hit the ground it immediately bounded up with his knee high in the air ready for another powerful stride. There wasn't the slightest trace of a back kick. The result was that from the side Charley looked as though he were running in a sitting-down position; his knees and feet were always out front. From the head-on or rear position, it looked as though he were fly-

Following pages: Wills/Wightman (USA) defeat McKane/Covell (GBR), Paris 1924

ing along two feet off the ground and never touching it. His feet rebounded with such speed that you couldn't see them hit the track.

Charley had no great early speed and won nearly all of his races by his explosive finish. His flying leap at the tape was of no value in gaining speed in the air, as he well knew, but it gave him a goal at which to aim.

As crowd pleasing as Paddock was, "The World's Fastest Human" actually won only a single gold medal. Indeed, his Olympic career was as rife with controversy as that of any runner of the time. Paddock came to Antwerp in 1920 as a heavy favorite to win both sprints. In his first final, the 100 meters, he followed his usual pre-race ritual, knocking on wood and then, once on the blocks, stretching his arms out as far as he could and slowly withdrawing them as the starter said "get set." Noticing Paddock's outstretched arms (already beginning to withdraw), the official ordered him to assume proper position and then immediately yelled "get set." This exchange confused Paddock's teammate Loren Murchison, who stood up, just as the official fired the gun, leaving the American well behind the pack. For the rest of the field it was a very close race, the lead changing hands several times, and was won only in the last few meters as Paddock leapt and broke the finish line with his chest. The 1920 Antwerp games saw Charley Paddock at his best, and the remainder of Paddock's Olympic career was not as successful.

The Olympic oath is administered to assembled athletes

Paris
1924

Fencers warm up in Stade Colombes Olympic

Olympic conditions couldn't have changed any more dramatically than during the twenty-four years that separated the 1900 and 1924 Paris games. In 1900 few Parisians paid much attention to the world-class athletes who had come to compete, and when they did it was to dismiss the strong, but often boisterous American team as *sauvages*.

That all changed by 1924. The United States was better trained and more carefully monitored as an athletic unit. It was also much larger than it had been in 1900. Its combined 320 athletes and support staff included 110 track-and-field performers, 20 fencers, 25 boxers, 66 swimmers, 11 gymnasts, 16 wrestlers, 10 team managers, 12 coaches, 10 trainers and 6 "rubbers." The ship on which this contigent arrived was a seagoing athletic transport with a cork running track, a swimming tank and boxing and wrestling rings.

The reception the team received also couldn't have been more different. The Americans were housed at Rocquencourt, the magnificent estate that had once been owned by Prince Joachim Murat, a marshal in Napoleon's army. And instead of being hooted at, the Americans found themselves called heroes. Their first night at Rocquencourt a fire raced through the neighboring village. Roused from their beds, the athletes lent their hands to the local fire department and later, upon learning that a fireman had been killed, raised $200 for his family.

The Americans were wildly cheered as they took the fields at the Stade Colombes Olympic. Unfortunately the team's performance did not completely live up to this reception. Indeed, at least in track-and-field, 1924 was Finland's great year. Five of that country's athletes accounted for a total of nine first-place finishes.

Left: Helen Wills (USA), singles champion. Right: Flora Black leaps scissors-style in non-Olympic meet.

Paavo Nurmi, after winning two golds and one silver in Antwerp, returned even stronger. To make matters worse for long-distance runners from other countries, Nurmi was joined on the Finnish team by Ville Ritola, a U.S. resident who was competing for his native country. Ritola, if not the equal of Nurmi, came very close to his teammate in talent and determination.

In a single week the two either together or separately entered six events. The first, the 10,000 meters, was held on Sunday, July 6. With Nurmi not running the race, Ritola won an easy victory, soundly beating Edwin Wide of Sweden. Three days later, Ritola won his second victory, the 3,000-meter steeplechase, a race Nurmi had not entered. Ritola's time set an Olympic record.

Thursday, July 10, was Nurmi's day, certainly the most amazing of his life, and probably of anybody else's in the history of long-distance running. The French, perhaps not thinking anyone would enter both events, scheduled the 1,500- and 5,000-meter races not only on the same day, but just half an hour apart. (When the Finns protested, the French lengthened the rest period to 55 minutes.) Nurmi, however, had practiced running the two races only minutes apart, and less than an hour after setting an Olympic record in the 1,500 he once again defeated Ritola, in the process setting another Olympic record, this time in the 5,000 meters.

Nurmi was still not finished. Two days later he won the cross-country race, setting another Olympic record. He and Ritola were also on the winning 3,000-meter team. In six races run over a span of eight days, Nurmi and Ritola

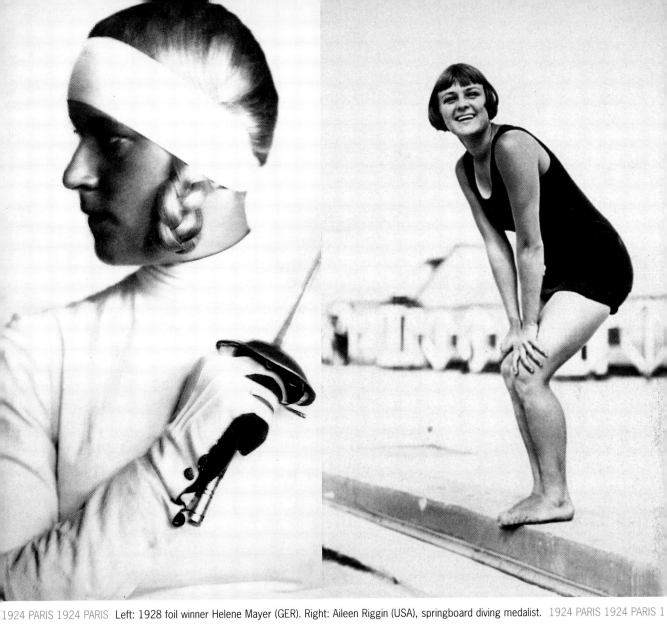

Left: 1928 foil winner Helene Mayer (GER). Right: Aileen Riggin (USA), springboard diving medalist.

not only collected six first places and two seconds, but they set one world record and three Olympic records.

Added to the medals won by these "Flying Finns," Finland enjoyed three more first-place finishes. Jonni Myyra won the gold, for the second time in a row, in the javelin. Another Finn, Eero Lehtonen, repeated his 1920 win in the pentathlon. And Albin Stenroos scored an upset in the marathon, a race he had not run in fifteen years.

The American team, so long accustomed to track-and-field dominance, did manage to produce at least a couple of standout performances. Harold Osborn won the decathlon and set an Olympic record in the high jump. (Even Jim Thorpe had not been able to win both the decathlon and an individual event.) And though the last of the Whales, Babe McDonald, had come to Paris as an honorary member of the team, Clarence "Bud" Houser upheld their tradition by winning the discus and the shot put, the last man ever to achieve such a double victory.

In the running events, however, the American team came up very short indeed. The United States did win both hurdle races, but managed only one victory in the flat races, the 200 meters. And even that success was tempered by disappointment. Charley Paddock, the veteran of so many close races, had been able to place only fifth in the 100-meter sprint two days before and thought his career as the world's fastest human to be over. The night before the 200, his friends Douglas Fairbanks, Mary Pickford and Maurice Chevalier tried to buck him up. He could win, they said, if he believed in himself. The next day Paddock took an early lead in the 200 meters final. Just before taking off in his standard finish-line leap, however, Paddock turned his head to check his opponents and teammate

American silver-medalist four-oared shell with coxswain team

Jackson Scholz shot past him for the win. After the race, Paddock was disconsolate. As Bud Houser later remembered, "He came up to me and said 'Bud, I'm so embarrassed I can't stand it. Will you walk up to the door of the stadium with me, and I'll run into the training quarters. I don't want to talk to anybody.'"

There were, however, a number of lighter and brighter moments for the Americans. Jack Kelly, the Philadelphia bricklayer who had won a gold medal in the single sculls at Antwerp in 1920 after having been barred from the prestigious Diamond Sculls race at the Henley Regatta (he was judged "unacceptable" because he worked with his hands) repeated, with his partner Paul Costello, his first-place finish in the double-sculls contests. The American team, one of whose members was the then unknown pre-med student Benjamin Spock, also easily won the eight-oared shell with coxswain race by more than 15 seconds, despite the fact that their stroke, Al Lindley, collapsed at the end of the race from nervous exhaustion.

The 1924 Paris games were also the occasion of a couple of farcical, albeit fairly serious disputes. Four months after a disputed Olympic sabre match, the Italian fencer Oreste Puliti fought an actual duel with the judge of that event, a Hungarian named Kovacs; the silliness ended when, after an hour or so, their seconds convinced them to shake hands. Then there was the middleweight boxing final, in which the Frenchman Roger Brousse was disqualified for biting his British opponent Harry Malin. Though Malin went on to win the medal, the British press was outraged at Brousse, "whose passion for raw meat led him to attempt to bite off portions of his opponents' anatomies."

106

Sculling triple gold medalist Jack Kelly (USA)

The 1924 games also marked the Olympic debut of one of the greatest, if not the greatest, freestyle swimmers of all time. Not only did American Johnny Weissmuller never lose an Olympic race, he never lost any race of any sort. In all he won a total of five Olympic gold medals. In Paris he finished first in the 100 and 400 meters and contributed to the team victory in the 4 X 200-meter freestyle relay, and also won a bronze medal in water polo. Four years later in Amsterdam he repeated his 100 meters and relay victories.

In addition to his superior skill Weissmuller had perfected what was known as the American crawl. In the early days of competitive swimming most contestants utilized a sort of combination dog paddle–breaststroke technique to propel themselves through the water. This changed late in the nineteenth century when an Englishman named Frederick Cavill observed South Seas Islanders swimming overhand and kicking their legs scissors style. This technique became known as the Australian crawl.

By the early twentieth century American coaches had modified this style by replacing the scissor kick with a straight-legged flutter technique. It was this new style, known as the American crawl, of which Weissmuller became the acknowledged master.

When his amateur swimming career ended, Johnny Weissmuller turned to Hollywood. In 1932 he started in his first of twelve "Tarzan" movies. Three other Olympic medal winners—freestyle winner Buster Crabbe, Herman Brix and decathlete Glenn Morris—followed Weissmuller in the Tarzan role.

107

American Johnny Weissmuller swims with his high-in-water, head-turning championship style

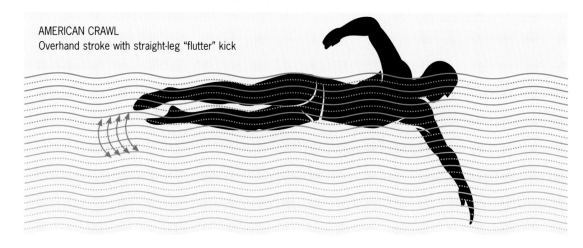

AMERICAN CRAWL
Overhand stroke with straight-leg "flutter" kick

AUSTRALIAN CRAWL
Overhand stroke with scissors-style kick

Harold Abrahams (GBR) glides to first-place finish in 100 meters

HAROLD ABRAHAMS AND ERIC LIDDELL

There is no need to embellish legendary Olympic accomplishments. Nor is it necessary to add color to the Olympic cast of characters. The simple fact that each is a world-class athlete given only one chance every four years to win an Olympic medal quite naturally places extraordinary men and women in unforgettable, even epic, situations.

For this reason, one of the best of Olympic movies, the fictional treatment of the 1924 games *Chariots of Fire*, in some ways misses the real drama underlying the accomplishments of its two main characters, the British runners Harold Abrahams and Eric Liddell. Abrahams's startling victory in the 100-meter sprint, for instance, had absolutely nothing to do with his disappointment at coming in third in the 200 meters. That race was actually run two days later. In truth, Abrahams's resolve to win the 100 meters was the result of months of hard work.

A year or so before the games Abrahams began to be coached by Sam Mussabini, who studied Abrahams and observed that his major difficulty was with his stride. Taking the coach's advice, Abrahams, using the sort of primitive sports technology available at the time, placed sheets of paper on the track exactly the correct stride length apart, then practiced by training his feet to land each time on these stride markers.

Even with all this preparation, Abrahams faced stiff competition in Paris. Charley Paddock, the world-record holder, qualified for the final, as did his two American teammates Jackson Scholz and Loren Murchison. But Olympic competitions very often seem controlled by the twin gods of providence and surprise. In other words, it was Abrahams's year. After twice tying the Olympic record of 10.6 seconds in his heats, Abrahams broke away from the

Right: Liddell (GBR), wins in 400 meters. Following pages: Harold Osborn (USA) in western roll style.

pack about halfway through the 100-meter final and strode steadily, almost coasted, to a solid victory.

The other now famous British runner associated with the 1924 games is the purportedly dour, devout Scotsman Eric Liddell. As portrayed in *Chariots of Fire*, Liddell learns upon arriving in Paris that the 100-meter sprint is to be run on Sunday and out of religious conviction refuses to enter the race, his specialty. Lord Burghley, the film story continues, gives his spot in the 400 meters to Liddell out of sympathy for his friend's dilemma. The problem with all of this is that hardly any of it is accurate. It is true that Liddell did refuse to run on Sunday, but he had been apprised of the schedule months before the Paris games. What the true Liddell story loses in filmic force, however, it gains in purely athletic drama. Like Abrahams, he trained rigorously for the 1924 games. Realizing that he could not run the 100, he prepared not only for the 200, another of his specialties, but also for the 400, a quite different sort of race. In that first race, the one which supposedly had so disappointed Abrahams, Liddell came in third behind Scholz and Paddock.

For the final of the 400-meters, however, he had a plan. When the gun went off, Liddell accelerated like the sprinter he was and ran the first half of the race in a time just $\frac{1}{10}$ second off his third-place time in the 200. This strategy seemed pure folly. Observers figured that Liddell would almost certainly falter. Remarkably he did not. In fact he ran the second half of the race in 25.4 seconds and finished at 47.6 seconds, 5 meters ahead of his closest competitor.

111

Amsterdam
1928

With Charles McIlvaine, American Paul Costello wins his third straight double sculls championship

The 1928 Amsterdam games were truly international in competitive scope, at least as evidenced by the wide distribution of gold medals. Not counting the smaller, poorly attended 1896 and 1904 games, for the first thirty years or so of Olympic competition the number of nations achieving first-place victories consistently hovered around fifteen. In 1928, however, of the forty-six countries represented (up two from 1924) twenty-eight claimed golds.

On the face of it, this change can be easily explained. In the past American athletes had routinely won the unofficial title as Olympic team champion. (In 1920 and 1924 the United States almost tripled the first-place totals of the runners-up.) At Amsterdam, however, the United States, while again coming in first in gold-medal victories, scored only twenty-two first place finishes, less than half of the forty-five it had accumulated in Paris in 1924.

The same was more or less true of many of the other nations used to strong showings on the gold-medal list. France, Great Britain, Italy and Sweden also saw their totals dramatically decrease. Even tiny Finland, which had made such a dramatic showing in Paris, won only eight golds, six fewer than in 1920.

Four years earlier Finnish officials, fearing that Paavo Nurmi was entering—and winning—too many events, had not allowed him to attempt to repeat his great Antwerp victory in the 10,000. Perhaps angered by this turn of events, Nurmi ran the 10,000 in Amsterdam, but after passing the 1924 champion Ville Ritola to win by 0.6 second, he stalked off the field, refusing to accept congratulations or even stand for a photograph.

Nurmi decided not to attempt to repeat his Paris victory in the 1,500. Instead, it was his countryman, indeed

Left: Women's high jump champion Ethel "The Saskatoon Lily" Catherwood (CAN)

a fellow from Nurmi's hometown, the twenty-two-year-old Harry Larva, who in the last 20 yards sprinted ahead of the French runner Jules Ladoumegue to win the race. The next day the 5,000 meters was run, and for a while it appeared to be a carbon copy of the 1924 race. Almost from the beginning Nurmi and Ville Ritola distanced themselves from the rest of the field, with Ritola, as he had done previously, holding the lead for half of the race. This year, however, Nurmi was unable to pass his longtime rival, and Ritola pulled ahead in the final lap to win by 12 yards.

As a valedictory of sorts, however, Nurmi entered the 3,000-meter steeplechase, an Olympic race he had never run before. And after their eight years of long-distance dueling, Nurmi and Ritola were once again the men to watch. But it appears that the strain of the 5,000, run just a day earlier, was too much. Ritola dropped out just short of the end of the race; Nurmi continued, but another Finn, Toivo Loukola, beat him by a full 60 yards.

Nurmi's losses were by no means the only upsets of the games. The American Joie Ray was expected to win the marathon, and indeed held the lead for half of the race, but at the end it was a completely unknown Algerian runner, Boughera El Ouafi, who won, outdistancing the field by 150 meters. And Miko Oda of Japan, another athlete unfamiliar to Olympic competition, won the triple jump, the first non-Westerner to win an Olympic event.

This is not to say that the unexpected always happened in Amsterdam. The American Bud Houser repeated his previous victory in the discus and the British runners Douglas Lowe and David Burghley won the 800 meters and the 400-meter hurdles, races in which they were the favorites. (Burghley had gained apocryphal fame by running

116

Center: Lord Burghley (GBR) wins 400-meter hurdles. Right: Ville Ritola (FIN).

around the Great Court in Oxford in the same amount of time it took the clock to ring out its twelve o'clock count.)

Along with the number of dramatic victories and losses, the Amsterdam games should also be remembered as the first in which women competed in track-and-field events. Five events were scheduled: the 100-meter sprint, won by the American Betty Robinson; the 4 X 100 relay, won by the Canadian team; the high jump, for which the gold medal was won by "The Saskatoon Lily," Ethel Catherwood, widely acknowledged as the most beautiful woman at the games; and the discus, first place in which was taken by a Polish athlete, Halina Konopacka.

But it was the last of these five events, the 800-meter run, which was the most controversial. Though the German Lina Radke won the race in world-record time, several of the runners-up dropped with exhaustion after the race. Deciding that such races were too strenuous for women, officials outlawed all women's races over 200 meters, a ban that remained in place for thirty-two years. There were no women's gymnastics at Amsterdam (these events would not be held until 1952), but the men's division produced one outstanding star, the Swiss gymnast Georges Miez, who won four gold medals and one silver. And in fencing, the Frenchman Lucien Gaudin became, after the 1904 champion Ramon Fonst, only the second man to take first in both the foil and epee.

Nothing, however, better epitomizes the competitive shocks and surprises of the 1928 games than the race rowed by Australian sculler Henry Pearce. In the lead in the single sculls final, Pearce stopped to let a line of ducks pass. He then put his oars back in the water and calmly rowed on to a five-length victory.

Robinson (USA) defeats Canadians Fanny Rosenfeld (left) and Ethel Smith (right) in 100 meters

BETTY ROBINSON

The first of a long line of female Olympic track-and-field stars was a sixteen-year-old Riverdale, Illinois, high school student named Betty Robinson. Robinson's running talent was discovered almost by accident when one of her teachers, after seeing the young girl take off to catch a train, asked to time her over 50 yards, which he did the next day in the halls of the school. Impressed by her near-record time, the teacher entered Robinson in a local indoor meet, one in which, to the young runner's surprise, she found herself competing with trained athletes from the Illinois Athletic Club. After finishing second to the club's star sprinter, Robinson was convinced to begin training seriously.

Later that spring Robinson ran for the first time in an outdoors meet, which just happened to be the Olympic tryouts for her section of the country. Robinson won her race in world-record time and after traveling to New Jersey for the national tryouts, won a place on the Olympic team by finishing second in the 100-meter sprint.

At Amsterdam Robinson, who was competing in only her fourth meet, was very nervous. "When I came onto the field," she remembered, "I discovered I had brought two left shoes . . . so I had to run back upstairs and get a right shoe." Robinson, however, had a strategy. "I had the feeling," she said, "if I got Fanny [Rosenfeld] on my right side so I knew where she was all the time, it would help." It apparently did help, for Robinson narrowly beat the Canadian. She also won a silver medal anchoring the 4 X 100 relay.

Three years after the Amsterdam games, Robinson was badly hurt in a plane crash and was expected never to compete again. Nevertheless, she returned to racing and won another silver medal at the 1936 Olympics.

118

Above: Williams (CAN) rests after 100 meters victory. Following pages: Start of middle-distance heat.

PERCY WILLIAMS

Prior to 1928 the majority of the world's best sprinters had been Americans. Of the fourteen Olympic sprints run so far (eight 100s, six 200s), only two winners, Reggie Walker and Harold Abrahams in 1908 and 1924, had not been American, and both of those victories had been upsets. The tradition of great American sprint champions, runners the likes of Archie Hahn, Ralph Craig and Charley Paddock, was expected to continue at Amsterdam.

But it was an extremely competitive group of international runners who were at the starting line of the 100 meters. Among the finalists was a practically unknown nineteen-year-old Vancouver student named Percy Williams, who had hitchhiked to the Canadian Olympic tryouts and had won himself a spot on the team. Despite the fact that he had equaled the Olympic record of 10.6 in his heat, Williams was given little chance to beat such a distinguished field. But after a couple of false starts, the Canadian immediately took the lead and finished comfortably ahead of the pack.

A day later Williams also qualified for the 200 meters final, lining up alongside what was perhaps an even stronger field. In the quarterfinals, he had come in second behind Helmut Körnig of Germany, who in winning equaled the Olympic record time of 21.6 seconds. (One of the favorites, the American Charlie Borah, came in third and was eliminated.) Williams then won his semifinal, just barely beating Walter Rangeley of Great Britain. In the final it was once again all Williams. Though Körnig initially led the race, Williams sprinted past the German and held off Rangeley to win by almost a yard.

119

S ANGELES 1932 LOS ANGELES 1932 Some 105,000 spectators watch opening ceremonies in Olympic Coliseum LOS ANGELES 1932 LOS ANGELES

Los Angeles 1932

Swedish team wins one of six races in 6-meter class yachting competition

The event-filled, multifaceted spectacle we now recognize as the Olympic games was invented slowly and steadily, almost piece by piece. Each games more and more nations participated, in effect enlarging and enhancing the competitive breadth. At that same time, the often chaotic panoply of individual athletic contests was abbreviated and standardized. By 1932, for instance, more than twenty-five of the track-and-field events run in the past had been changed, and an Olympic meet was shaped pretty much as it is today.

But the achievement of the organizers of the Los Angeles Olympics, one which set a benchmark for many Olympics to come, was in the massive, detailed and ultimately spectacular administration of the entire event. A huge stadium with seating for 105,000 spectators was built and—even more importantly—filled every day. Indoor events were held in another new building, a 10,000-seat Olympic auditorium.

The new swimming pool was surrounded by bleachers capacious enough to hold 12,000 people. Shooting events had their own site; rowing and sailing races were staged in Alamitos Bay, where seats were erected for 12,000 spectators. Finally, a self-sustaining pocket-size municipality, with its own postal address—Olympic Village, U.S.A.—was constructed to house the male athletes. (Female athletes stayed in Los Angeles hotels.)

To make matters even better, the various competitive venues were beautifully constructed. The track, for instance, was so fine that one athlete said he felt as if he was "running on a springboard." These perfect conditions, enriched by what one observer described as "California's far-heralded golden clime," led to an unprecedented num-

123

István Pelle of Hungary in gold-medal pommel horse performance

ber of record-breaking performances. In twenty-two track-and-field events alone, nineteen Olympic records were set, seven of which doubled as world records.

Each heat in the sprints, it seemed, was run faster than the previous race. The American Eddie Tolan, for instance, knocked a full half a second off Percy Williams's 1928 100 meters time and almost as much (0.4 second) off Archie Hahn's twenty-eight-year-old Olympic record in the 200 meters.

That the 400-meter race was won in world-record time came as no suprise. Ben Eastman of Stanford was generally acknowledged as the fastest man in the world at that distance and at 800 meters. During the spring season immediately preceding the games he had run this race, as well as its sister race, the 440 yards, in record-breaking times. But the longtime Olympic coach Lawson Robertson of Penn apparently felt personally challenged by Eastman's coach, Dink Templeton, and convinced his sprinter, Bill Carr, to train for and enter the 400 instead, which he did, unexpectedly defeating Eastman to win the gold in this longer distance.

Despite the fact that Eastman was not in the 800 meters, a world record was also set in that race: Thomas Hampson beat the favorites, Alex Wilson and Philip Edwards, by less than a foot. The most peculiar world record, however, was set in the 400-meter hurdles. Robert Tisdale of Ireland had spent much of the year prior to the Olympics training for the games. The trouble was that he had no regulation-size hurdles. In addition he arrived in Los Angeles sick and exhausted from his trip across the world. Tisdale did make the finals and was holding a solid

lead when he tripped over the last hurdle. Regaining his balance, he just managed to break the tape ahead of the American Glenn Hardin. Olympic rules at the time, however, specified that knocking over a hurdle disallowed Olympic records, and silver medalist Hardin, who finished the race 0.2 second behind Tisdale, was named the new world-record holder.

Records, both Olympic and world, were also set in the longer distance races, but this time not all by the Finns, who had practically owned these events for the past twenty years. The Finnish runner Volmari Iso-Hollo did win the 3,000-meter steeplechase, but with Finnish champions Paavo Nurmi and Ville Ritola both declared professionals and thus unable to compete, the rest of the long-distance events were won by runners of other nations: Luigi Beccali of Italy scored an upset victory in the 1,500, as did Poland's Janusz Kusocinski in the 10,000 and the Argentinian Juan Carlos Zabala in the marathon.

The female star of the track-and-field was Mildred "Babe" Didrickson from Texas. Her record-setting performances in three different events electrified the crowd.

Newly emerged as an Olympic power was Japan, which sent 142 athletes to Los Angeles, second only to the United States in the size of its squad. Given their relative inexperience in Olympic track-and-field events, the Japanese did exceedingly well, repeating that country's 1928 victory in the triple jump as well as placing in a number of other events.

USA men's field hockey team plays India, winner of six consecutive golds (1928–56)

But it was in swimming that Japan really shone, winning and placing in every single race except the 400-meter freestyle, which was won by Buster Crabbe, the American swimmer who went on to follow in Johnny Weissmuller's footsteps playing Tarzan in the movies. Since many of the Japanese victors were very young (1,500-meter gold medalist Kusuo Kitamura, for instance, was only fourteen at the time), it appeared that a dynasty resembling that of Finland's in track was in the making, and indeed Japanese swimmers did very well in Berlin in 1936. World War II intervened, however, and 1932 remained the height of Japan's swimming dominance.

The boxing and wrestling matches, held in the new Olympic auditorium, also produced some outstanding performances. The Swedish wrestler Ivar Johannson won the middleweight freestyle championship, fasted for four days and returned to the arena to win the gold medal in the Greco-Roman welterweight final.

In boxing, the Argentines won both the light-heavyweight and heavyweight titles. Apparently not satisfied with their ring performance, the Argentines spent so much time pummeling each other on their trip home that upon arrival their heavyweight champion Santiago Lovell was arrested and hauled off to jail.

The Los Angeles games were so successful across such a broad spectrum that one of the most popular of the world-class venues was the banks of Alamitos Bay. In fact, it is estimated that 80,000 people lined the banks of the bay to watch the final of the eight-oared shell with coxswain, which was won by rowers from the University of California with a dramatic 0.2 second lead over the Italian national team.

In controversial 5,000 meters final, Lehtinen (FIN) beats Hill (USA) by 3 inches

In men's field hockey, India was unstoppable, humiliating the United States by a score of 24–1, the most goals ever scored in international competiton. Field hockey is a fairly ancient game, versions of it having been traced from ancient Egypt and Greece through the Middle Ages, when the Araucano Indians of Argentina are said to have played a similar game called *cheuca*. But the rise of contemporary field hockey is most often associated with Great Britain, where it grew out of several analogous games: Irish hurling, Scottish shinty and Welsh banty.

In field hockey eleven players on each side play two 35-minute halves and maneuver a baseball-sized hard-wood ball with hooked, waist-high sticks flattened on only the striking side. Goals can be scored only if the ball is shot within the "shooting circle," which is scribed 16 yards from the goal. Because of these rules, field hockey is in large part a passing game. Generally passes have been of two sorts: long hits to an open man favored by British and Continental players and shorter, more accurate pinpoint passes typical of the Indian style of the game.

It should come as no surprise that field hockey was first introduced as an Olympic sport in 1908 by the British, who easily won the gold medal that year. (Indeed, of the first four finishers three were English teams and the fourth was Irish.) But though the French, Danes and Belgians fielded competitive teams at Antwerp, it was India, a British colony at the time, that turned out to be the great world power in field hockey. In its first Olympics in 1928, the Indian team, lead by Dyan Chand, the so-called Babe Ruth of field hockey, won the tournament without giving up a single goal.

S 1932 LOS ANGELES 1932 Left and middle: Double medalist Babe Didrikson hurls javelin. Right: Disqualified for improper technique, Didrikson loses

BABE DIDRIKSON

Babe Didrikson was lauded and admired by fans and sportswriters in about equal proportion to the extreme dislike and utter disparagement privately expressed by her fellow teammates. Didrikson was no doubt an enormously gift-ed athlete. Myth measured against myth, her legendary 1932 performance as a member of a track team fielded by the Employer's Casualty Company of Dallas, Texas, at least matches, if not outshines, that of Jim Thorpe.

While Thorpe had help against the Lafayette College track team, Didrikson was in fact the the only member of her squad and thus did in actuality beat the entire Northwestern University team to single-handedly win the U.S. Women's Track-and-Field Championship.

Didrikson, like Thorpe, excelled at almost any sport in which she competed. After the Olympic Games, she played for the touring House of David baseball team and once as a lark pitched for the Philadelphia Athletics in an exhibition game. She also was a superb golfer, once winning seventeen tournaments in a row. Indeed, comparisons with Thorpe were made by many sports fans. In 1950 when he was voted the best male athlete of the half century, Didrikson took the honors as the best female athlete for the same period.

But Didrikson was never shy about any of these accomplishments. It appears she was at heart a relatively good-humored rube from Texas, albeit one who walked with a swagger and was wont to brag and boast. Didrikson came to the Evanston, Illinois, Women's A.A.U. Championships, which doubled as the 1932 Olympic trials, skilled in any number of events. (Against Northwestern she had won both throwing and running contests.) Her performances

...np to Jean Shiley. Following pages: Finish of four-oared shell with coxswain. Women's fencing match outdoors in Coliseum. LOS ANGELES 1932 LOS A...

at the A.A.U. meet qualified her for five spots on the Olympic team. But Olympic rules limited her to three, and Didrikson chose to compete in the javelin, the high jump and the high hurdles.

The first of these events she won with one throw, even though the javelin awkwardly slipped out of her hand. It appeared that she would win the 80-meter hurdles just as easily. In her heat she tied the world's record, but in the final she false-started and then managed to beat the second-place finisher, Evelyne Hall, by only inches.

Didrikson's next and final event was the high jump. Here too she had strong competition. Back in Evanston she tied for first place in this event with a young suburban Philadelphia girl named Jean Shiley, who had the good fortune to be coached by the famous Lawson Robertson. After Didrikson's first two gold medals, she was apparently more boastful than usual and her teammates had about had their fill of her. (Her incessant harmonica playing seems also not to have endeared her to her fellow athletes.)

The night before the high jump final, all the female track-and-field athletes went to Shiley's room, urging her to defeat Didrikson. But as in Evanston, Didrikson tied Shiley, each woman jumping a world's record height of 5' 5¼". A jump-off was scheduled, but after the first jump the Olympic judges awarded the victory to Shiley, pointing out that contrary to the rules, which stated that a jumper had to take off on one foot and land on the other, Didrikson was allowing her shoulder to precede her body across the bar, a clear violation.

LIN 1936 BERLIN 1936 BERLIN 1936   The last of 3,000-person relay team carries Olympic torch into the stadium   BERLIN 1936 BERLIN 1936 BERLIN 1

Berlin
1936

Medal ceremony for 400-meter relay

It is easy to stagelight the 1936 Olympic Games with the high-intensity kliegs of world politics. The city of Berlin was home to the Nazi party. Adolf Hitler, his arm elevated in an open-handed salute, was the presiding host. Soldiers marched in the streets. Flags emblazoned with symbolic political imagery hung everywhere about the city.

In the past, international athletics had evoked an amiable sort of chauvinism. Now the realpolitik of world affairs shaped the decisions of many Olympic teams. The Spaniards, in the midst of their own impending civil war, stayed home. After its defeat of Ethiopia, Italy sent athletes to Berlin. The French government debated whether to withdraw support of its team as a protest against fascism but decided, reluctantly, to send a team. And the United States, after much soul-searching about Hitler and his racial policies, concluded that the games would still be basically apolitical and resolved to compete.

But to view the Berlin Olympics as a grim, politically driven games is to ignore the athletes themselves, almost all of whom remember the 1936 competitions mostly as a lot of fun. Indeed, even before the first event was staged, controversy erupted not over ideological differences but because of an excess of high spirits. Eleanor Holm had, since winning the 1932 gold medal in the 100-meter backstroke, lived what some considered a wild and dissipating Hollywood lifestyle. After qualifying for the 1936 games she continued to have a good time even on the ship carrying the American team to Berlin. This irked American Olympic officials, and after discovering Holm passed out in her cabin after an evening of drinking and playing craps, they kicked her off the team. The swimmer protested, to

135

Germany's gold medal four-oared shell team gives Nazi salute

no avail, and spent her Berlin days, and nights, continuing to celebrate and generally having a grand time.

Somewhat ironically, the upshot of Hitler's obvious attempt to impress the world was that the 1936 games were probably the best staged up to this point in Olympic history. The Germans spent a reported $30 million building a new stadium, a beautiful swimming pool and a dozen or so other sites. The Olympic village even surpassed the one constructed in Los Angeles in its ability to accommodate athletes. Francis Johnson, a member of the first Olympic basketball team, remembers "just killing time" in the village when Hitler and his companion Eva Braun came through on a tour. Hitler, Johnson has said, "was just like you or me or anybody else standing there with his girlfriend"—no big deal. What Johnson recalls as more important was the basketball final. The Germans, clearly not understanding the game very well, staged it outside on a clay court, which after a soaking overnight rain became so slick that "you'd just slip and slide along." (The U.S. team beat the Canadians for the medal by a score of 19–8.)

The 400-meter gold medalist Archie Williams was even more forthright about the absence of grim, political solemnity in Berlin. "One thing about the whole thing," he has said, "was that we were having a lot of fun." Williams was one of those American athletes insultingly called the "black auxiliaries" by the Nazis; another was Cornelius Johnson, who after winning the high jump was ignored by Hitler, who did not congratulate most winners. But it was not a political snub that stuck in Williams's memory; rather it was "Ol' Corny's ability to psyche out opponents by not even bothering to take his sweat suit off until the bar was set over 6 feet 6 inches."

136

One of Forest "Spec" Towns's favorite memories of the games was John Woodruff's incredible victory in the 800 meters. Woodruff had planned to control the race by setting a rather slow pace, thus enabling him to kick to victory in the last lap. But every time he slowed up, Phil Edwards, the Canadian, would pass him. Finally, Woodruff regained the lead then simply stopped, creating a bottleneck out of which he sprinted to win the medal.

Woodruff also remembers the nature of the games as less politically charged than has been suggested, at least as far as the athletes were concerned. It is a well-known story that Hitler refused to acknowledge the victories of the black star of the games, Jesse Owens. Woodruff said that tale is "fiction."

And in many cases, the Germans were more trouble on the field than on the soapbox. Hans Woellke ended virtual American domination of the shot put, and Karl Hein won the hammer throw. In women's swimming a German, Hendrika Mastenbroek, won three gold medals and one silver. And in women's fencing a German-born American resident, specially recruited by the Nazis despite her Jewish heritage, narrowly lost the individual foil title to the Hungarian Ilona Schacherer (later Elek).

There was, however, an athletic event with direct and rather ironic political reverberations. The marathon was won by a young Korean, Sohn Kee-Chung, who because his nation had been conquered by Japan was running under the Japanese flag. Sohn was not given a chance to repeat his victory in the next Olympics, even though they were scheduled for Tokyo. Actual war, not athletic conflict, saw to that.

Peruvian goalie leaps above Austrian players in disputed soccer quarterfinal

SOCCER

The game of soccer, it seems, has historically always had a boisterous, somewhat crowd-rousing element in its makeup. In the fourteenth century King Edward II banned the sport in England after players routinely rampaged through the centers of towns, pushing, kicking, smashing and advancing the ball in any way they pleased. But soccer would not die that easily, and by the nineteenth century, with its rules standardized and much more civilized, it had become a nationally recognized and accepted game in Great Britain.

Soccer was the first team sport included on the Olympic program. These matches were not without the problems commonly associated with the game. In 1924, for example, several fans were injured as a result of overcrowding. Once World Cup competition was instituted in 1930, the line between amateur and professional players had become so indistinct that soccer was dropped from the Olympics in 1932. Though the Germans returned soccer to the games in 1936, it had lost none of its rather rowdy and contentious elements.

The worst of these fan excesses occurred during the hotly contested quaterfinal match between Peru and Austria. During the second overtime the Peruvian fans stormed the field and attacked several Austrian players. Amazingly enough, the game continued during all of this mayhem, and taking advantage of the confusion Peru scored twice. The Austrians, of course, protested, and a new game was rescheduled; but by this time the entire Peruvian team had withdrawn from Olympic competition, leaving Austria to battle it out with Italy in the final, which the Italians won in overtime by a single goal.

138

Ludwig Stubbendorff (GER) in the three-day equestrian event aboard his mount, Nurmi

THREE-DAY EQUESTRIAN

The three-day event is probably the toughest of all Olympic equestrian challenges. The first part of the competition is the dressage, in which the horse is required to perform a series of twenty movements, each designed to showcase the athletic abilities of horse and rider. The second day comprises the rather complicated and demanding endurance run. This race is broken up into four stages, labeled A through D. In A the horse must trot over a marked and timed course. Next is Phase B, the steeplechase. Phase C much resembles A, except that now the horse must canter. Phase D, the final event, is the cross-country jumping contest, conducted over a course dotted with fences, ditches, hillocks and other such obstacles.

One of the heroes of the 1936 Olympics three-day equestrian team event was the German army Lieutenant Konrad von Wangenheim. During phase B of the event von Wangenheim's horse, Kurfurst, pulled up at the fourth obstacle, throwing its rider to the ground. Despite suffering a broken collarbone in the accident von Wangenheim, in order to keep his team in the race, remounted and finished that part of the event.

The next day, in the cross-country phase of the competition, Kurfurst reared up and fell on top of the already injured lieutenant. For a few dramatic seconds von Wangenheim didn't move; then all of a sudden he stood up, remounted and, remarkably, finished the event without making another fault.

Though von Wangenheim and his horse amassed more penalty points than all his teammates combined, the German team won the three-day event, coming in 200 points ahead of its nearest competitor, Poland.

Helen Stephens (USA) defeats rival Stella Walsh (POL) in 100 meters

HELEN STEPHENS

Stella Walsh, the Polish-born runner who took the 100-meter sprint in Los Angeles in 1932, was fast; but Missourian Helen Stephens, "The Fulton Flash," was even faster. In the first of their match races, Stephens easily beat the Olympic champion, a defeat that rankled Walsh. After the race she grumbled that Stephens had gotten an early start, but the outspoken winner shot back, "Come to Fulton, and I'll run you over plowed ground and give you an even break." The next time the two raced against each other was not in a farm field but in the finals of the 100 meters in Berlin, where again Stephens coasted to an impressive victory.

Stephens's other great distinction in Berlin was that she was the only American athlete to be invited to Hitler's private box. At first she and her coach were not sure what to do, but finally both decided that there would be nothing wrong with accepting the invitation. "Well," Stephens has said, "immediately Hitler goes for the jugular vein. He gets a hold of my fanny, and he begins to squeeze and pinch and hug me up, and he said, 'You're a true Aryan type. You should be running for Germany.'" Stephens also met German minister Herman Goering in even more embarrassing circumstances. At a post-games party for gold medalists Stephens was asked to go upstairs to see Goering. "This black thing he had on was his kimono," Stephens remembered, "and he was sitting there in his shorts." She fled. After her remarkable victories, Stephens was accused by a Polish official of being a man, a charge that was completely untrue. As it turned out the finger had been pointed at the wrong runner. Many years later, after her death, it was discovered that it was Stella Walsh who was actually a man.

Stephens with Jesse Owens, against whom she later ran exhibition races

JESSE OWENS

The first fifteen years following the 1936 Olympics were tough ones for Jesse Owens. True, he had won four gold medals in Berlin, and true, he had been greeted back in the United States by ticker-tape parades in New York and Cleveland, but once the initial excitement died away, there was very little Owens was able to do. For a while he worked on Alf Landon's presidential campaign. He then was paid to run exhibition races against such things as horses and motorcycles. Finally he took a low-paying job as a playground instructor in Cleveland.

Not until the 1950s, when he turned to public speaking and began his career as what one called "a professional good example," did Owens begin to reap the benefits of his Olympic victories. In many ways, this post-Olympic pursuit could have been predicted simply by looking at his performance and behavior in Berlin. Owens had even then been a role model, albeit as an amateur rather than as a professional.

Indeed his performance on the track and field could be described as easygoing, congenial, sunny even. Owens had always been a great athlete. A year before Berlin he had broken five world records and tied another at the Big Ten Championships. And though his sprinter teammates Ralph Metcalfe and Frank Wycoff were great runners, once on the field in Berlin for his first final, that of the 100 meters, Owens breezed to victory, almost as if he were running alone without a worry in the world.

Two days later, his good nature gained him an unexpected ally during the long jump competition. Owens was amazed when officials counted what he thought was a warm-up jump as his first attempt. Admittedly nervous, he

141

Above and right: Jesse Owens sets Olympic record in long jump

fouled on his next jump. That left him with only one qualifying leap. As he was composing himself, the German jumper Luz Long came up to Owens and asked what was wrong. "Something must be eating you," he continued, "you should be able to qualify with your eyes closed." And there the two chatted, in full view of Hitler and the Nazi-filled stands, until Long suggested that Owens take off a few inches behind the line, thereby avoiding the danger of another fault. Owens took the advice, qualified, and later that same afternoon easily defeated his new friend with a final leap of 26' 5½".

Owens went on to win the 200 meters two days later with equal ease. Though his teammate Mack Robinson, the brother of future baseball great Jackie Robinson, had matched his trial time of 21.1 seconds, Owens absolutely ran away with the final, beating Robinson by a full 4 yards.

Though Owens, along with most of his teammates, was not congratulated by Hitler after his victories, the only real controversy that rose up around him had nothing to do with his skin color. Olympic coach Lawson Robertson decided that the American 4 X 100-meter relay team was not fast enough to beat the competition. He first replaced Marty Glickman with Owens and then Sam Stoller with Ralph Metcalfe. The suggestion was made that Stoller and Glickman, both of whom were Jewish, were supplanted as a sop to Hitler's anti-Semitic views. The 800-meter gold medalist John Woodruff discounts that reasoning: "Hitler had nothing to do with our team." Whatever the reason, the new quartet won easily, and Owens collected his fourth medal of the games.

Following pages: Owens on the run, heading home victorious. Finish-line judges await start of race.

ATHLETIC VERSATILITY

Jesse Owens's multiple gold-medal showing was not unprecedented in Olympic history. From the very first staging of the modern games, many athletes had garnered more than one first-place victory. In 1896, for instance, four contestants won more than one event. This tradition continued throughout the early history of the games.

As a general rule, however, multiple medalists did not mix events. They were exclusively runners or throwers or jumpers. True, there were several exceptions. Martin Sheridan, for instance, won medals in discus and standing jump contests. And certainly Jim Thorpe was an excellent all-around athlete and could conceivably have trained himself to be competitive in single-event competition. There was also that other great athletic talent of the early games, Babe Didrikson, who either won or placed in throwing (javelin), running (80-meter hurdles) and jumping (high jump). And in addition to winning a combined five first places in freestyle races, Johnny Weissmuller was also in 1924 a member of the American bronze-medal-winning water polo team. Similarly, Aileen Riggin, who in 1924 took two firsts in springboard diving, also came in third in the 100-meter backstroke.

By 1936, however, most Olympic athletes specialized in one specific category of event. Indeed, in future years there were very few who attempted to repeat Owens's double event victories. Had the scheduling been different in 1948, Fanny Blankers-Koen might have won both the sprints and the long jump; but not until Carl Lewis equaled Owens's feat in 1984 and Jackie Joyner-Kersee won both the heptathlon and long jump in 1988 did one athlete prove himself or herself to be the best in the world at two related but different athletic skills.

CITIUS ALTIUS FORTIUS

LONDON 1948 LONDON 1948 LONDON 1948   Guardsmen in ceremonial busbees enter Olympic stadium   LONDON 1948 LONDON 1948 LONDON 19

London
1948

Unidentified vaulter breaks pole during qualifying round

The 1948 Olympic games more resembled those held in Antwerp in 1920 than those staged by the British twelve years earlier in London. Both Antwerp and London 1948 were postwar games, charged with the virtual resurrection of Olympic competition after it had temporarily succumbed to the pressures of world events. Both also were plagued by spells of bad weather and often adverse track-and-field conditions.

Great Britain, like almost all the countries of Europe and the Far East, was still very slowly recovering from devastations of World War II. Money was scarce. But the British did the best that they could, and on the unusually hot morning of July 29, 1952, a little more than four thousand athletes from fifty-nine nations marched into Wembley Stadium. Significantly absent were athletes from Germany and Japan, nations which had been barred from competition, and those from the Soviet Union, which had not as yet joined the Olympic community.

The first event, the running of the 10,000 meters, saw the first of several dramatic upsets of the games. Finland's current world-record holder, Viljo Heino, was the heavy favorite to win the 10,000. But as had happened in Antwerp when Paavo Nurmi won his first Olympic medal, a new champion, the Czech army lieutenant Emil Zátopek, appeared on the scene. Not only did Zátopek beat Heino, but his pace was so fast that the Finn dropped out of the race and by the end of the race Zátopek had lapped all but two runners and won by a huge 300-meter margin.

Another 1948 upset was predicated upon a previous unexpected defeat. The American Harrison "Bones" Dillard was widely considered the best hurdler in the world, but during the final of the 110-meter Olympic tryouts he

Wrestler Gazanfer Bilge (TUR) defeats Ivar Sjoin (SWE) in freestyle featherweight championship

knocked over the first fence, stumbled, knocked over two more and stopped about halfway into the race. Fortunately, Dillard had earlier qualified for the 100-meter sprint, a race he won in London, beating, among others, his teammates Barney Ewell and Mel Patton in record time. (Patton made up for his loss by winning the 200 meters.)

Similarly, the outcome of the 800-meter run had a direct effect upon the 400 meters. After having narrowly lost to Mal Whitfield in the longer race, the Jamaican runner Arthur Wint mentally prepared himself for the 400-meter duel with his teammate Herbert McKenley, the "surest sure thing of the games." McKenley, as had been expected, took an early and fairly large lead but for some reason he began to slow, and about 20 yards from the finish line Wint caught his countryman and went on to win by 0.2 second.

Kayaking had first been introduced as an Olympic sport in Berlin before the war. London saw the appearance of the all-time Olympic kayaking medals champion, the Swedish paddler Gert Fredriksson, who in the next twelve years went on to win six golds, one silver and one bronze medal. Similarly in yachting, Paul Elvström of Denmark won the first of his four successive gold medals in the Finn class.

In weightlifting, the story was a contrast of big and small. Despite having arms so short that they barely reached above his head, the 4' 10" American Joe Di Pietro won the bantamweight crown. His teammate, the super heavyweight gold medalist John Davis, was so big and strong that between 1938 and 1953 he never lost a weight-lifting contest of any sort—indeed, in no competition was anyone able to defeat him in the press, snatch *or* jerk.

150

Forced to switch hands due to a war injury, Karoly Takacs (HUN) wins pistol gold

Weight also played a part in the boxing tournaments. The flyweight boxing champion Pascual Perez of Argentina was almost disqualified for being overweight when officials mistook him for his teammate, the bantamweight Arnoldo Pares. Coincidentally, Pares was also judged to be overweight. After a series of futile attempts to lighten the boxer by cutting his hair and scraping dead skin off the soles of his feet, it was discovered that the problem was not with Pares but with the scales.

In wrestling, the national championship was a split decision between Sweden, whose athletes won a total of thirteen medals, including five golds, and Turkey, which counted six first places, four in the freestyle competitions and two in Greco-Roman style wrestling, among its eleven medals. Remarkably, the Turkish super heavyweight gold medalist Gyula Bobis had begun his wrestling career as a more than one-hundred-pound lighter flyweight.

Perhaps the most mentally disciplined athletic feat performed in 1948 was the victory of the Hugarian shooter Karoly Takacs in the rapid-fire pistol contest. Prior to the war, the right-handed Takacs had won the world championship in this event, but while serving in the army a grenade exploded in his shooting hand, practically blowing it off. Takacs painstakingly retrained himself to shoot with his left hand—well enough to win an Olympic medal.On the final day of the games the sun came out. The games had been a fine recommencement of international athletic competition. Though the second half of the twentieth century would not begin for another two years, the 1948 Olympics could be said to have served as a precursor of all the uninterrupted games to come.

151

Decathlon champion Bob Mathias (USA) winds up to hurl winning discus throw

BOB MATHIAS

If Bob Mathias had been any older or more experienced when he took the field in London to compete in the decathlon, he might, as he once said, have been "intimidated." But Mathias was only seventeen years old. He knew hardly anything about the Olympics, as the last Olympic competition had been staged in 1936, when he was five years old.

Mathias also knew hardly anything about the decathlon, having previously participated in only two such competitions, both within the month before he arrived in London. In high school, he had thrown the discus and shot put and had dabbled in the hurdles and the high jump, but he had never run the 400- or 1,500-meter races, thrown the javelin or pole vaulted. Before his first decathlon he practiced these new events, but as he has said, "My times in the longer races were terrible.... At the time the philosophy was to work on the first nine events then just gut it out in the 1,500 meters. Everybody did it that way because the conventional wisdom was that if you trained for the distances, you would hurt yourself in the other...events. The coaches felt that way about weightlifting so we were not allowed to touch [weights] because they would make you muscle-bound."

All of these factors became apparent in the first event of the day. Mathias was not only unused to the 16-pound shot (12 pounds was the high school weight), he was unaware that it was against Olympic rules to leave the throwing circle from the front. In spite of fouling on his first attempt, he did, however, manage to use his remaining put to throw the shot farther than his competitors. The high jump also gave him trouble. His first two leaps were ter-

Mathias competes in two of his strongest events, the pole vault (left) and the long jump (right)

rible. But he regained his composure and finally jumped 6' 1¾". Indeed, Mathias did well enough in the other three events, the 100 and 400 meters and the long jump, to end the day in third place.

The following day was almost disastrous for Mathias. The weather was awful and as he was part of the second group of decathletes to compete, his events lasted well into the night. Additionally, after he threw the discus, his single best skill, an official mistakenly picked up the flag marking Mathias's distance; after searching the rain-soaked field for half an hour officials gave Mathias an estimated distance of 144' 4".

By the time it was his turn to pole vault, the bar could just barely be seen in the twilight. Then it turned very dark, so dark that officials had to shine a light on the javelin foul line in order for Mathias to see it at all. But at each of these events Mathias shone, and despite running an abysmally slow 5:11 in the final event of the day, the 1,500, Mathias won the decathlon—his third decathlon of the month, and of his life.

Mathias returned to Olympic athletics in 1952, winning the Helsinki decathlon by a record-setting 800 points. Later he enlisted in the Marines and retired from athletics. Mathias had previously made a movie, *The Bob Mathias Story*, and after leaving the service he had several bit movie parts and played opposite Jayne Mansfield in a film about the 1896 Olympic marathon victory called *It Happened in Athens*. Mathias was best known in later years as a U.S. congressman from California. After his electoral defeat in 1974, he became associated with the U.S.O.C., serving as the first director of the Olympic training center.

153

Blankers-Koen (HOL) dominates the 200 meters (above) and leaves the muddy field victorious (right)

FANNY BLANKERS-KOEN

It is possible that Francina "Fanny" Blankers-Koen was the greatest female track-and-field performer of the first half of the twentieth century, greater even than Babe Didrikson. True, Didrikson proved herself to the best all-around athlete. No one before or since has displayed so many skills in so many sports. But on the track and on the field it is interesting to imagine a scratch duel between the two.

Blankers-Koen, at least on paper, was the faster of the two. Indeed, her speed may even be more impressive given her age. When Didrikson competed in Los Angeles she was a twenty-one-year-old typist barely out of school. Blankers-Koen also competed in the games at a young age. In 1936, as an eighteen-year-old, she ran the sprints in Berlin, where her best finish was fifth in the 400-meter relay, and also tied for sixth place in the high jump competition. But then war intervened and by the time she was next able to enter Olympic competition, Blankers-Koen was a married thirty-year-old woman with two young children. Notwithstanding her age and responsibilities, she entered five events, the 100-meter and 200-meter sprints, the 400-meter relay, the 80-meter hurdles and the long jump.

The first of these events, the 100 meters, she won easily, by 5 yards. The 80-meter hurdles, however, was a more exacting race. Before the final Blankers-Koen, as had been her custom, was extremely nervous. Her principal opponent was the British athlete Maureen Gardner, acknowledged as one of the premier female hurdlers in the world.

Gardner took an early lead in the final, and in an attempt to overtake her, Blankers-Koen crashed her way

154

Following pages: Boxing ring at Wembley. Austrian javelin gold medalist Herma Bauma.

across the last hurdle and practically fell across the finish line. After conferring a few minutes, the judges named the Dutch hurdler the victor. Blankers-Koen's time was 11.2, a full half-second faster than Didrikson's 1932 time of 11.7.

It is more difficult to compare the leaping ability of the two athletes. Though Didrikson's high jumping performance in Los Angeles remains controversial, Blankers-Koen's long jumping skill is indisputable. Unfortunately in 1948 the qualifying heats for the hurdles and long jump were scheduled for the same afternoon, and the Dutch athlete chose to compete in the former. There is little doubt, however, that had she been able to compete in the long jump she would have won, the winning distance of that year's Olympic competition being a full 20 inches shorter than Blankers-Koen's world record.

One thing the two athletes did not share was a similar temperament. Unlike Didrikson, who was brash, cocky and sure of herself, Blankers-Koen, even after winning both the hurdles and the 100-meter sprint, was so nervous before the 200 meters final that she came close to withdrawing. Her coach-husband, Jan Blankers, calmed her, and she won the race by almost 7 yards.

In addition, Blankers-Koen did not, as had Didrikson, capitalize on her fame. After winning her fourth gold in the 4 X 100-meter relay, she returned home to her two children, and though she did continue to compete, she was most often seen pedaling her bike around the streets of Amsterdam.

155

Release of pigeons during Helsinki opening ceremony

Helsinki
1952

Women javelin throwers prepare for competitions

It was raining, and the magnificent, new, red-cinder running track circling the Helsinki Olympic stadium had already been chewed up by the feet of the nearly six thousand athletes from sixty-seven nations marching in to participate in the thirteenth Olympics. In the stands seventy thousand spectators awaited the arrival of the Olympic flame, the progress of which from Greece had been the subject of considerable political controversy. For the first time in its history the Soviet Union had decided to send athletes to the games, but for some unaccountable reason it rejected the request that the Olympic flame be allowed to pass through its satellite nation of Estonia.

Yet the Finns refused to let anything political spoil the ceremonial opening of the games. Another route was chosen, and as those assembled in the stadium turned toward the entry tunnel, in jogged a short, slight, balding man: the greatest runner in Finnish history, Paavo Nurmi. After igniting the Olympic flame, the fifty-five-year-old champion turned and handed his torch to another Olympic medalist, sixty-two-year-old Hannes Kolehmainen, who then ascended the steps of a 272-foot tower and lighted a second blaze.

Indeed, despite the common view that these games were a sort of ex-officio Cold War, pitting the United States against its enemy, the Soviet Union, the results of competition during the Helsinki Olympics were, as usual, fundamentally based on athletic skills, not political leanings. In no event was this more true than in one which pitted an American F.B.I. agent against a Russian adversary. Though jokes were made about the Russian following the American rather than vice-versa, Horace Ashenfelter defeated Vladimir Kazantsev in the 3,000-meter steeplechase.

159

Left: Pole vaulter gold medalist Bob Richards. Right: 10,000-meter walk bronze medalist Bruno Junk (SOV).

Though Soviet women won the shot put and the discus, the majority of Soviet medals were amassed in events such as wrestling and gymnastics. In gymnastics in particular there were two outstanding Soviet performances: Viktor Chukarin, dubbed Viktor the victor, won the men's all-around championship, and Maria Gorokhovskaya placed first in the women's competition.

In most ways, the great stories of the Helsinki games were those featuring surprise defeats. For instance, George Brown of U.C.L.A., widely favored to win the high jump, fouled out. Then there was the upset winner of the 100-meter sprint, Lindy Remigino of Manhattan College, who when asked if he now deserved to be called the world's fastest human, responded, "Are you kidding? I'm not even the best sprinter we have."

Of course, a number of events turned out exactly as expected. Harrison Dillard, who had in 1948 failed to qualify in the 110-meter hurdles, won his specialty in Olympic-record time. Bob Mathias repeated his victory in the decathlon, this time by the largest margin in Olympic history. The Reverend Bob Richards, the silver medalist in the pole vault in London, leapt 14' 11" to win the first of his two golds. And the Brazilian triple jumper Adhemar da Silva won the first of his two successive golds by breaking his own world records four times in the finals.

Two of the men appearing in the boxing finals would in the future become very famous indeed. Four years after the Helsinki Olympics, Floyd Patterson, the shy, seventeen-year-old middleweight winner, captured the professional heavyweight championship of the world. Patterson held this title until 1959, when he was knocked out by the Swede

Left: Javelin champion Dana Zátopek (CZE). Right: Parry O'Brien prepares for winning shot put.

Ingemar Johansson, a fighter who, ironically, in the Helsinki super-heavyweight final was so obviously afraid of his opponent, H. Ed Sanders, that he backpedaled around the ring to avoid being hit until he was disqualified.

Some Olympic events seldom draw international attention and acclaim. This is a shame, given the outstanding skills and accomplishments of the athletes competing in those contests. In Helsinki Karoly Takacs, the veteran who had been forced to switch shooting hands after a war injury, once again won the rapid-fire pistol competition. A change of handedness also figured into the training of the winner of the 1952 individual epee tournament. Edoardo Mangiarotti's father, the Italian fencing master Giuseppe Mangiarotti, had converted his young son to a left-hander. The elder Mangiarotti believed that this shift would benefit the boy in matches with right-handers—which it apparently did, since by the end of his Olympic career Edoardo accumulated a total of thirteen medals.

In swimming no single individual stood out as the great star of the games. Instead there were a number of singularly outstanding performances. The American Clark Scholes set an Olympic record in the preliminary heat of the 100-meter freestyle, as did his teammate Ford Konno in the 1,500-meter freestyle final. The Hungarian Valeria Gyenge defeated world-record holder Ragnhild Andersen-Hveger in the women's 400-meter freestyle race.

Two of the most remarked upon people at the Olympic pool were not even swimmers. When Joan Harrison of South Africa won the 100-meter backstroke, her coach fainted. And Jean Boiteux, after winning the 400-meter freestyle, found himself being hugged by his father, who had jumped, clothes and all, into the water.

161

American springboard diving gold medalists Pat McCormick (left) and Sammy Lee (right)

SAMMY LEE, PAT McCORMICK

The Helsinki diving competition featured two athletes, one male and one female, who would in their Olympic careers collect a total of one silver and six gold medals. Of these two, Pat McCormick, winner of both the springboard and the platform diving competitions at Helsinki, was the quieter and more self-effacing. At Helsinki divers often complained about the conditions. Spectators were too close to the pool, they said, and the frogman/photographer swimming around unnerved them. In spite of these distractions, the fearless McCormick amazed judges by performing dives that were at the time only attempted by men.

Because she was pregnant in 1955 it was assumed that McCormick would pass up the 1956 Melbourne games. But by continuing to swim and train almost to her due date, McCormick surprised all by arriving at the games, eight months after giving birth, and easily repeating her double victory. Another of McCormick's children, her daughter Kelly, also became a diver; her style and grace reminded people of her mother, and she finished second in the springboard competition in Los Angeles in 1984 and third in the same event in Seoul in 1988.

The other great gold medalist of the Helsinki games was Dr. Sammy Lee, the skilled and sometimes irreverent Korean-American winner of the platform dive in 1948 and 1952. All he had to do to win first place, he thought, was to complete his famous forward three-and-a-half somersault. "All I can remember," Lee said, "is hitting the water and it tingled all over—like when you take a belly flop. I thought, My God, what did I do? I came to the surface, and I saw a 10, 9½, 9½, 9 and a 7. I knew it was all over, and for the second time in history a man walked on water."

Above: Zátopek leading in 5,000-meter final lap. Following pages: Diver Sammy Lee (USA) jokes at poolside.

EMIL ZÁTOPEK

To watch Emil Zátopek run was to witness two different running styles. From the waist up he seemed to be in agony. He was described variously as looking like he had been "stabbed in the heart" and as "clawing at his abdomen in horrible extremities of pain." But despite this almost comic thrashing of his arms and tossing of his head, Zátopek's legs strode so steadily ahead they seemed to be driven with the mechanical regularity of an automaton.

A Czech army officer whose only duties were to train for athletic competitions, Zátopek arrived in Helsinki having won two medals in London: gold in the 10,000 meters and silver in the 5,000. His first race in 1952 was the 10,000, which he won by over 100 meters. Since he was next scheduled to compete in the grueling marathon, observers were surprised to see him out on the track for the 5,000-meter trials. His explanation: "The marathon contest won't be for a long time yet, so I simply must do something until then." This playfulness extended to his heat. Late in the race Zátopek slowed down, flagged four runners following him ahead, and trotted to the finish line alongside the eventual fourth-place finisher, Bertil Albertsson, all the while engaging in conversation with the Swede.

Zátopek also won the final of the 5,000 in fairly dramatic fashion, sprinting around the leaders on the final turn and dashing across the finish line well ahead of the pack. That afternoon Zátopek's wife, Dana, took first in the javelin, prompting him to joke, "At present, the score of the contest in the Zátopek family is 2–1. To restore some prestige I will try to improve on it—in the marathon race." Which he did, rather easily. Indeed so effortlessly that one of his post-race comments was typically Zátopekian: "Marathon is a very boring race," he said.

1956 MELBOURNE 1956   Olympic torch lit for the first time in the Southern Hemisphere by Australian distance runner Ron Clarke   MELBOURNE 1956 M

Melbourne 1956

Laszlo Papp (HUN), winner of 3 Olympic titles: middleweight (1948) and light middleweight (1952, 1956)

Home-field advantage is a concept common to competitive sports. Aided by the comfort of familiar surroundings and cheered by partisan fans, the theory goes, athletes step up the level of their performances. With the possible exception of the Berlin games, this benefit had traditionally not been obvious during the previous Olympics: Greeks had not dominated in Athens in 1896, French athletes had not been the big winners in either of the Paris games and even the Finns had scored best not in Helsinki but in Paris and Amsterdam.

In many ways, the Melbourne games were the exception to this odd Olympic tradition. Australian athletes won significantly more medals than they had in past games. In the first ten Olympics, the country had averaged about five golds, silvers and bronzes combined. In the post–World War II games they did better, doubling the number of combined awards to twelve. But in 1956, on their home fields, gymnasia and swimming pools, the Australians almost tripled their best showing, garnering a total of 35 medals and coming in third behind the Soviet Union and the States in the unofficial team competition.

It is probably unprovable that the performances of Australian athletes can be explained by the fact that their country was that year's Olympic host, but if this did at least contribute to their successes, the advantage was almost lost in pre-games political wrangling. Australian politicians spent so much time fighting each other over Olympic funding and venues that barely over a year before the games were scheduled to begin, little in the way of construction and preparation had been accomplished.

Left: Decathlon winner Milt Campbell (USA). Right: Vladimir Kuts (SOV), 5,000- and 10,000-meter gold medalist.

In the end, however, the Australians pulled together and sites were readied. But then there arose two other, quite different problems: international politics and the weather. As the games were set to begin Hungary revolted against the Soviet Union and there was some question about whether Hungarians would be able to compete. About the same time Israel invaded the Suez, and as a protest Egypt, Lebanon and Iraq withdrew. Mainland China, angry at the inclusion of Nationalist China, also refused to send athletes.

Then there was the weather, which initially was terrible. Since Australia is in the Southern Hemisphere, the games were held not in July or August but in late November and early December, which in Australia is not really summer but more like late spring. Fortunately, the cold, wet weather that greeted the athletes upon arrival softened into early summer and most competitions were unaffected by meteorological conditions.

Whatever the effect of all of this upon the international athletes, it is undisputed that the Australians did extremely well. In men's and women's swimming Australia won eight golds, four silvers and two bronzes. Then there were two extraordinary Australian runners, Betty Cuthbert and Shirley Strickland.

Cuthbert at seventeen was the younger of the two, but against her very fast, world-class opponents in the 100-meter run Cuthbert won by 0.2 second. In the 200 meters Cuthbert was again the winner, equalling an Olympic record. In her last race, as the closer in the 4 X 100-meter relay, Cuthbert led her team to a new world record. One of Cuthbert's teammates in that race was the twenty-seven-year-old Strickland, who a few days earlier had bettered

Left: Roger Bannister, first to break 4-minute mile. Right: Ál Oerter (USA), wins first of 4 golds in discus.

Fanny Blankers-Koen's world record in the 80-meter hurdles. (Blankers-Koen, hobbled by injuries, dropped out of the finals.)

As great as the contingent of athletes that represented Australia was, the country did suffer some disappointments, most notably in the high jump. The nineteen-year-old American Charlie Dumas had earlier that spring become the first man to officially break the 7-foot barrier. The Australians, who also had a high jump champion, Charley Porter, publicly expressed annoyance when Dumas did not bother to practice before the competition. But in the finals, despite Porter's jumping 2 inches higher than he ever had before, the laid-back Dumas calmly and quietly took the gold.

As usual, Americans did very well in other track-and-field events. The devoutly religious Bobby Joe Morrow, who thought it unethical to anticipate starts, won the 100-and 200-meter sprints and anchored the victorious 4 X 100-meter relay team. Tom Courtney won the extremely exciting 800 meters final by sprinting steadily in pursuit of the leader Derek Johnson and winning by 0.1 second. After this race, Johnson commented, "My head was exploding, my stomach ripping, even the tips of my fingers ached. The only thing I could think was, If I live, I will never run again."

In both men's and women's throwing events the accomplishments of the athletes were admirable if somewhat predictable. In the men's throwing events, the Americans were as powerful as they had been early in Olympic his-

In last leg of winning 4 X 100-meter run, Betty Cuthbert (AUS) pulls up on Heather Armitage (GBR)

tory. All three gold medalists set new Olympic records: Parry O'Brien won his second gold in the shot put by almost a foot; Al Oerter also received the first of his four gold medals in the discus; and Hal Connolly soundly defeated his Soviet rival in the hammer throw. In women's throwing, the Soviets also repeated their dominance, losing first place only in the discus.

The great Russian performer in the games was the long-distance runner Vladimir Kuts. Though he also won the 5,000 meters, the 10,000 was Kuts's greatest race and perhaps the most exciting of the games. Kuts took off at the start and set a terrifically fast pace. By the middle of the race his only competition was the Briton Gordon Pirie, who hung on at Kuts's heels. To get rid of Pirie, Kuts tried a couple of tactics: he first sprinted ahead at a murderous speed then slowed and attempted to force Pirie to set the pace. Neither of these maneuvers worked. Close to the end of the race Pirie was still there. In desperation, Kuts practically stopped, forcing Pirie to step around him. With only a few laps to go Kuts passed his opponent and dashed to a first-place finish. (Pirie, so exhausted from the duel, finished eighth.)

The one team that had more than an athletic motive to defeat the Russians was that of the overrun Hungary, which had come to Melbourne in order to avenge military and political defeat. This anger came to fruition in the Hungarian-Soviet water polo match, which was so patently violent and bloody that referees had to abort the contest and give the Hungarian team, then leading 4–0, the victory.

Gold medalist Hal Connolly (USA) sets Olympic record, defeating rival Mikhail Krivonosov (SOV)

HAL AND OLGA CONNOLLY

In the practice days prior to actual competition the American hammer thrower Hal Connolly and the Czech discus champion Olga Fikotová began the most improbable of romances. After the games, a seemingly inconsequential flirtation led to a controversial marriage not only between two athletes but between two different political cultures.

Fikotová was a very gifted young athlete, having played on the national women's basketball team before taking up the discus. She easily emerged as the clear victor in the discus in Melbourne, beating, among others, the 1952 gold medalist Nina Ponomaryeva (Romaschkova).

Knowing Olga had won her event the day before only added to Connolly's desire to beat his longtime opponent, Mikhail Krivonosov, with whom he had dueled in the hammer during the past year, each in succession outthrowing the other for new world records. He did finally edge out his rival with a throw of 207' 3".

At the end of the games the lovers had decisions to make. Connolly's friend, the Reverend Bob Richards, told him, "You better get her to stay, or it's good-bye." But Connolly and Fikotova considered her family and her continuing medical studies and decided that she would return to Prague. After the games, Connolly obtained a visa to visit Czechoslovakia, and with the help of Emil Zátopek and his wife, Dana, Hal and Olga married. Later the two convinced the Czech government to let them return to America. Both continued to compete in the Olympics, he in 1960, 1964 and 1968 and she through 1972. The marriage eventually ended in divorce. Neither, however, had any regrets; Olga in fact called their union and her eventual American citizenship "the very essence of the Olympic dream."

171

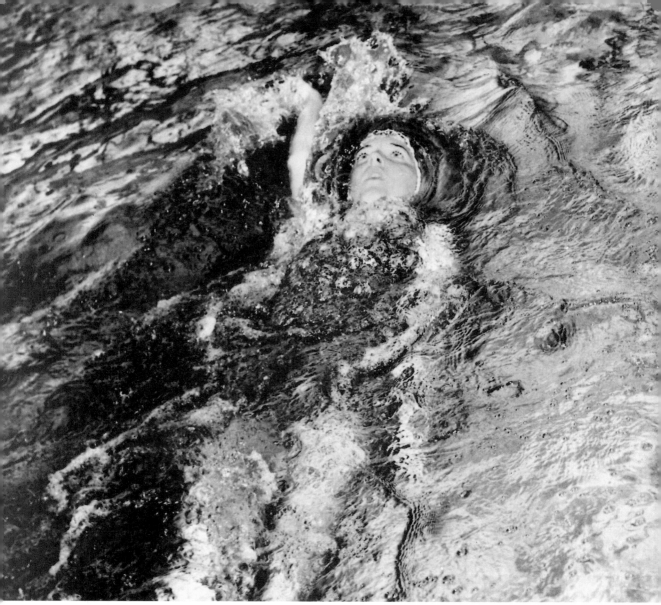

Above: Maureen Murphy (US) places in backstroke. Right: Dawn Fraser (AUS) sets 100-meter freestyle record.

AUSTRALIAN SWIMMERS

For some reason Australians at Melbourne had no great skill at either swimming backward or breaststroking or but-terflying forward. But at propelling themselves headfirst through the water as fast as possible, Australian swimmers were at the 1956 Melbourne Olympics clearly far superior to swimmers from any other part of the world.

Perhaps the Australian predilection for this event derived from the fact that the preference of most freestylers was one or another version of that overhand, leg-extended kick method commonly called the Australian crawl. But even though this speedy method of swimming was discovered, if not invented, in Australia, swimmers from that country had never before won an Olympic gold medal.

True, a few Australian freestylers, such as Frank Beaupaire and Andrew "Boy" Charleton, were world-class swimmers, but until 1956 none had been judged the fastest in the world in their specialties. Additionally, what is remarkable about the 1956 Australian group is that most were in many ways all-around freestylers. Take the two gold medal relay teams, for instance. At Melbourne, each male swimmer in the relay swam 200 meters, a distance generally considered as reserved for sprinters.

Not so on the Australian team. True, Jon Henricks and John Devitt had placed first and second in the 100 meters. But the third and fourth swimmers, Murray Rose and Kevin O'Halloran, had come in first and fourth in the 400-meter race. Additionally Rose had won the 1,500, a race usually considered entirely different in both skill and strategy.

The members of the winning women's 4 X 100-meter relay race were equally talented, and even more out-spoken and colorful. Dawn Fraser, who took the lead leg, had beaten her teammate Lorraine Crapp in the 100-meter race, even though in the first of the trials Crapp had lowered the Olympic record by an amazing 2 seconds. When it was Fraser's turn to qualify she in turn had lowered Crapp's time by a full second.

Despite this time, the seventeen-year-old Fraser was nervous about the upcoming match with Crapp. The night before the final she dreamed, as she has said, that "I had honey on my feet and it was hard to pull them off the starting blocks. . . It seems a long time before I hit the water, and it wasn't water; it was spaghetti. Of course I fouled up at the turn and took a few mouthfuls, and I woke up gasping and fighting in a sea of spaghetti." In spite of her sticky pre-race nightmare Fraser overcame an early Crapp lead to defeat her teammate. In third place was Faith Leech, also a member of the relay team.

Six days later it was Crapp's turn. At the time, Crapp was the world record-holder in the 400 meters; the first woman to break 5 minutes. Fraser kept up with her friend for the first third of the race, but Crapp had greater endurance at this distance and ended up defeating Fraser by 8 seconds. Crapp's time was not quite world-record speed, but it did set an new Olympic mark.

In sixth place in the 400 was Sandra Morgan, and later that week, she, Fraser, Crapp and Leech broke the world record in the 4 X 100-meter relay by two seconds.

173

ME 1960 ROME 1960 ROME 1960 ROME 1960   U.S. team en route to opening ceremony of 1960 games   ROME 1960 ROME 1960 ROME 1960 ROM

Rome
1960

Olympic marathoners pass the Roman Colosseum

That the Olympic Games are a modernized continuation of an ancient tradition was nowhere better symbolized than in Rome in 1960. The Italians had been preparing for the games for years; indeed, they were so far along in 1956 that Olympic officials, faced with the early difficulties of the Australian preparations, briefly considered transferring that year's games to Italy.

Architecturally, the Roman athletic venues were a spectacular mixture of the old and the new. Several of the sites, including the beautiful main stadium, the Stadeo Olimpico, were designed by the Italian modernist architect Pier Luigi Nervi; other events were staged in centuries-old structures. The gymnastic competitions, for instance, were held in the Baths of Caracalla site, and wrestling matches were conducted outdoors in the Basilica of Maxentius.

The one problem the Italian organizers could not overcome by means of perfect preparations was the Roman summer. Most of the more than five thousand athletes from eighty-four nations—a record year for participation—were in attendance. The majority of these competitors, however, were unaccustomed to the extreme heat and humidity of Rome. Indeed, it is recorded that at least one athlete, the British walker Donald Thompson, trained by filling his bathroom with pots of steaming water, shutting the door and exercising as long as he could in this muggy, stifling meteorological equivalent of the upcoming competitive conditions.

As it turned out, most athletes were not materially affected by the weather. The Australians, fresh off their triumphs four years earlier, came to Rome with hopes of repeating their 1956 victories. Rome brought instead

Left: Larissa Latynina (SOV), winner of 18 medals in gymnastics

mixed and sometimes unusual results. Swimmer Murray Rose did win the 400-meter freestyle but lost to teammate John Konrads in his attempt to repeat in the 1,500. And John Devitt, who had won the silver medal in the 100-meter freestyle in 1956, now captured the gold.

There were really quite bizarre reversals involving members of the Australian women's swimming team. The great swimmers Dawn Fraser and Lorraine Crapp had always exhibited colorful if not slightly rebellious personalities. In Rome, however, both, at least in the eyes of Australian team managers, went slightly over the top. Fraser, after winning the 100-meter freestyle race and thinking she did not have to compete for several days, went out on the town. The next afternoon when she was reminded to ready herself for the relays, she refused, citing her wasted physical condition. Her teammates were furious and refused to speak to her for the remainder of the games.

Crapp's conduct also got her into difficulties. Having been married shortly before the games, she requested that she be allowed to stay with her new husband off the Olympic village site. When this request was denied, Crapp went right ahead with her plans and snuck out each night to meet her husband, despite the fact that overly zealous Australian officials had put her under special watch. Depressed by what she considered her imprisonment, Crapp swam so poorly that in the relay she actually gave up her team's lead to Carolyn Wood, a member of the unexpectedly victorious American team.

All was not discord and controversy on the Australian track-and-field team, however. Herb Elliot, the current

Center: Karpati (HUN) defeats Ravagnan (ITA) in sabre semifinal. Right: Silver medalist Polina Astakhova (SOV).

world-record holder in the 1,500-meter race, pushed himself so hard in the final—never turning around to notice that he had a 20-meter lead—that he broke his own record. Two other athletes from Down Under, albeit from New Zealand rather than Australia, also scored impressive victories. In the 800-meter run, Peter Snell was given little chance to defeat the world-record holder, Roger Moens of Belgium. At the tape, however, Snell was even with Moens and, as he has said, "by hurling every ounce of effort into the finish, and flinging myself forward," he scored one of the most impressive upsets of the games. Snell celebrated by watching his teammate Murray Halberg compete in the 5,000 meters. Halberg's strategy was to begin his sprint on the third-to-last lap. This he did, gaining a huge lead, but the sprint totally exhausted him and he barely managed to hold on to the lead before collapsing across the finish line, the tape clutched in his hand.

One of the tensest races of the games was the 100-meter sprint. The German Armin Hary had been often accused of cheating on the start by jumping the gun, but after false-starting twice he leaped into the lead and won by what has been described as a "long foot." The German did not compete in the 200 meters, a race also plagued with false starts, which was won by the sunglasses-wearing Italian Livio Berutti.

As a whole, despite the sometimes extreme heat, track-and-field performances in Rome were quite strong. Though hammer champion Hal Connolly did poorly due to a pre-games injury, hurdler Lee Calhoun repeated his 1956 victory. And after the retirement of Bob Richards, American pole-vaulter Don Bragg coasted to victory.

Rafer Johnson (USA) and Yang Chuan Kuan after decathlon 1,500-meter

Bragg's off-the-field ambition (perhaps obsession) was to play Tarzan in the movies; after being declared the gold medalist he beat his chest and released a booming Tarzan roar.

Ralph Boston, who just prior to the games had broken Jesse Owens's world record in the long jump, defeated an extremely strong field of competitors by leaping one centimeter farther than the second-place finisher, Irvin "Bo" Roberson. The decathlon, which throughout had been a duel between the American Rafer Johnson and the Taiwanese C. K. Yang, was won in the darkness of the last day of the event. Johnson, though finishing 6 seconds behind Yang in the 1,500, managed narrowly to beat his rival on points to take the championship.

In 1960 the Soviet Union was, as usual, extremely strong in the wrestling, fencing and gymnastics competitions. The all-around gymnastics championships were won decisively by Boris Shakhlin and his female teammate Larissa Latynina. The Press sisters, a pair of Soviet track-and-field athletes, were also noteworthy, both for their victories (Irina won the 80-meter hurdles and Tamara won the shot put) and for the fact that after sex tests were instituted by international officials in 1968, both chose to retire gracefully.

The Rome Olympics ended with the marathon, the finish line of which was directly beneath the ancient Arch of Constantine. Though it was a strong, varied field, the surprise winner was the barefooted Ethiopian palace guard Abebe Bikila, who relaxed after the race and said happily, "I could have kept going and gone around the course another time without difficulty. We train in shoes, but it is much more comfortable to run without them."

180

Triple-medalist Wilma Rudolph wins 100 meters by 0.3 second

WILMA RUDOLPH

As a child Wilma Rudolph gave no indication that she would develop into a world-class runner. In fact, her family worried whether she would ever walk. The twentieth of twenty-two children born into a poor Tennessee family and weighing only 4½ pounds at birth, Rudolph remained unhealthy most of her childhood. In rapid succession she came down with double pneumonia, polio and scarlet fever. Though her left leg was tightly bound in a metal brace, Rudolph nonetheless loved sports and managed to play ball, hobbling awkwardly, with her brothers.

Whether it was determination or exercise or a combination of the two, by the time Rudolph was eleven she was able to walk unaided. Even more miraculously, at the age of sixteen she could not only run, but ran well enough to qualify for the Olympic team. In Melbourne she earned a bronze as a member of the 4 X 100-relay team.

After the games Rudolph continued her athletic career, both in track-and-field and in basketball. Just prior to graduating high school, however, she became pregnant. After the birth of her baby, Rudolph entered Tennessee State University, where she was the mainstay of that school's women's track team, the Tigerbelles. In the 1960 Olympic trials Rudolph set a world record in the 200-meter sprint.

In Rome, however, heading onto the field for her first heat in the 100 meters, Rudolph sprained her ankle. But she was still unflappable—if it had not been for a slight wind, Rudolph's winning time in the 100 meters would have broken a world record. In the 200 meters she set an Olympic record. And in the finals of the 4 X 100-meter relay, Rudolph made up time lost by a teammate's bad pass and won her third gold medal of the games.

181

Left: Richard Cochran, III (USA) takes third in discus. Right: Light-heavyweight champion Clay.

PARRY O'BRIEN

Throughout the 1950s Parry O'Brien had been the world's preeminent shot putter. He may also have been the most competitive athlete this sport had ever seen. As a student at U.S.C., many nights O'Brien snuck into the darkened Los Angeles Coliseum, just to get the Olympic feel. He also developed the "O'Brien style" of putting the shot: he faced the back of the throwing circle, adding momentum to his hop and thrust. After winning the gold medal at Helsinki in 1952, O'Brien was unbeatable, winning 116 meets in a row. He also became the first man in history to put the shot over 60 feet. In Melbourne, O'Brien repeated easily, and his distances that year were so superior to the competition's that only one man, his teammate Bill Nieder, could match even O'Brien's shortest put.

O'Brien did not like to lose. But between the Melbourne and the Rome games, he was finally defeated, notably by his longtime rival Nieder. According to Nieder, "It griped O'Brien so much that he wouldn't speak to me." But if O'Brien did not talk to Nieder, he did talk about him. "Nieder is a cow-pasture performer," he has been quoted as saying. "He can't stand the pressure." This feud continued right through the 1960 Olympic trials, when Nieder narrowly missed making the team due to very strong performances by Dallas Long and Dave Davis. Soon the initial two-man squabble spread throughout the shot-put squad. Despite placing fourth in the trials, Nieder's pre-games performances were so commanding that he replaced Davis. During the first few puts in Rome, O'Brien completely outdistanced his opponents, but Nieder, on his last attempt, wound up and put the shot an astounding 18 inches farther than O'Brien's longest throw, spoiling the champion's chance at a third straight Olympic title.

182

Following pages: Marathon-winner Bikila enters Arch of Constantine. Men's 400-meter intermediate hurdles.

CASSIUS CLAY

Cassius Clay was by every account one of the most popular people in the Rome Olympic village. With camera in hand the eighteen-year-old Louisville, Kentucky, light-heavyweight boxer roamed around, introducing himself to the athletes of other countries, taking their pictures and posing with them when asked.

Clay won his gold medal with ease and expeditiousness. He knocked out his first opponent in the second round and defeated the next two boxers by unanimous decisions. Finally, in a fashion for which he would become famous, he toyed with Zbigniew Pietrzkowski for a couple of rounds in the final, dancing and backpedaling, before so over-powering his rival in the last round that again the judges' decision was unanimous. But for all the nonchalance with which he had won it, Clay was enormously proud of his gold medal. He was also proud to be an American. When goaded by a Russian journalist about the lack of black rights in his home country, Clay shot back: "Russian, we got qualified men working on the problem . . . America is the greatest country in the world, and as far as places I can't eat goes, I got lots of places I can eat—more places I can than I can't."

Unfortunately, one of the eating places closed to Clay was the scene of an ugly incident. After the games Clay and a friend were refused service at a Louisville restaurant, even though the champion introduced himself and showed the waitress his medal. Clay and his buddy left, chased by members of a motorcycle gang. Picking a fight with the Olympic boxing champion was not the best idea to enter a motorcyclist's mind. The outdoor boxing match was soon over and Clay, disgusted and depressed, chucked his gold medal over the rail of a nearby river bridge.

183

Japanese youth, born on the day Hiroshima was bombed, holds Olympic torch

Tokyo
1964

折返点

Abebe Bikila (ETH), first man to win two successive Olympic marathons

One of the great pleasures of individual Olympic competitions, for participant and fan alike, is that they have never been predictable. Pre-games favorites walk away defeated as often as they mount the stand to receive medals. Wholly unknown athletes gain fame as regularly as they remain uncelebrated.

But if the outcomes of particular events have usually been impossible to forecast, there has developed over the years certain national sporting traditions: the Americans had as a rule been strong in track-and-field; the Turks had always been competitive in wrestling; and after the start of their participation in the Olympics, the Soviets quite often won the majority of gold medals in men's and women's gymnastics.

In 1964 one of the longest of these traditions ended. Though fencing had never threatened to take the spotlight away from other more popular events, it had been a continuing feature of the Olympic program since the revival of the games in 1896. For the most part, the French and the Italians had been the most consistent winners in fencing, with one notable exception—the sabre category. For sixty years the Hungarian sabre team had won every gold medal in this event. In 1964, however, despite the Hungarian Tibor Pezsa taking first place in the individual sabre, the team victory went to the Soviet Union. On the grand scale of Olympic moments this defeat was hardly noticed, but to the Hungarians it was an alarming and demoralizing turn of events, almost a national tragedy.

Episodes such as the Hungarian team's loss had always been seen as only a tear in the weave of the grand Olympic tapestry, and that incident's overall effect on the larger 1964 games was certainly no exception. The

TOKYO 1964 TOKYO 1964 TOKYO 1964 Japanese gymnast Shuji Tsurumi, silver medalist on the pommel horse TOKYO 1964 TOKYO 1964 TOKYO 19

Japanese put on exceedingly well-run games. Over $2.8 billion were reportedly spent overall, and preparations were so meticulous that the opening ceremonies were actually rehearsed beforehand, with 70,000 schoolchildren used as stand-ins for athletes and spectators.

The athletes stepped confidently into the flow of these smoothly run games and turned in a series of dramatic and memorable performances. On the first day of competition the unknown American Billy Mills won the 10,000-meter race. Several days later, there was another upset, this time in the 5,000 meters. After Ron Clarke of Australia, the overwhelming favorite, wore himself out early in the race, Harold Noprath of Germany, William Dellinger of the United States, Michel Jazy of France and Kip Keino of Kenya jockeyed for the lead. Behind them was the American Bob Schul, who began to sprint with about 300 meters left. Boxed in, he managed to push past Keino, and running the last 300 meters in 38.7 seconds, an absurdly fast time, crossed the finish line with a lead of 0.2 second.

A similar race had been run by the obscure New Zealander Peter Snell in 1960 when he scored a major upset in the 800 meters. In 1964 Snell, considered a favorite, won the gold in both the 800 meters and the 1,500 meters, the first time anyone had won both events since Mel Sheppard in 1908. And even though he was not the clear-cut favorite, 1960 marathon champion Abebe Bikila repeated his victory so easily that he was able to show the crowd how fresh he was by jumping up and down in clowning warm-up exercises.

In the final round of the high-jump competition it appeared that Robert Shavlakadze and Valery Brumel, both

Soviet high-jumper Valery Brumel ties American John Thomas, but wins gold on fewer tries

of the Soviet Union, and John Thomas of the United States were about to be eliminated. All three, however, made their next jump easily. At 7' 1" Shavlakadze missed and was out. The bar was raised ¾". John Rambo of the United States, who had kept up with the leaders, also missed, leaving Brumel and Thomas, who made that height, tied. At 7' 2½" the two leaders knocked the bar over, and though their best jumps were identical, Brumel, having made fewer misses, was awarded the gold.

The great rising performer of the women's track-and-field was the nineteen-year-old Tennessee State star Wyomia Tyus, who earned the title of the world's fastest female by winning the 100-meter sprint in world-record time. In Rome in 1960, the women's 800-meter run had been, after a lapse of thirty-two years, again listed on the Olympic schedule. But the most exciting running of this newly reinstated race took place in Tokyo, where the Briton Ann Packer, after almost opting out of the event to go shopping because she ran poorly in her heats, won decisively, coming from behind to break the tape 5 meters ahead of second-place finisher Maryvonne Dupureur of France.

Earlier in the week Packer's teammate Mary Rand had earned the distinction of being the first British woman to win an Olympic gold medal by leaping a world-record distance in the long jump. Tamara Press, the great Soviet thrower, was also back for the Tokyo games, triumphing in both the shot put and the discus—her last Olympic medals, as it turned out.

In swimming, there were some large disappointments and disagreements among the consistently strong

189

American Joe Frazier takes super-heavyweight boxing title

Australian team. After an argument between Australian officials and 1964 medalist Murray Rose about whether he should return home from college in California to try out, the perennial champion was not allowed to compete. Then there was the ever colorful and troublesome Dawn Fraser. After capturing the gold medal in the 100-meter freestyle in Olympic-record time, Fraser decided as a prank to sneak into the Japanese emperor's palace and steal a flag. She was caught, and Australian officials, apparently having had quite enough of Fraser, banned her from competition for ten years.

In rowing, the eight-oared shell with coxswain of the Vesper Boat Club of Philadelphia won a narrow victory over the favorite, the very strong German team. The race was not without physical repercussions for both teams. As Emory Clark, a member of the American team, remembered, he was so drained that he managed only "to crawl out on the deck on my hands and knees." As for the Germans, they were even more worn out: "It took them half an hour to get their boat out."

Clark's other fond memory of the Tokyo games was his friendship with the American boxer Joe Frazier, a poor young man from North Philadelphia who impressed Clark with his good humor, courage and endurance. After winning the heavyweight final, Frazier appeared wearing a cast on his right hand. Clark asked his new friend what had happened. Replied Frazier, "I broke my hand fighting the Russian in the semi-final, but I didn't tell anybody because I knew they wouldn't let me fight."

Billy Mills (USA) defeats Mohamed Gammoudi (TUN) in 10,000 meters.

BILLY MILLS

To be an unknown, an underdog, simply by virtue of the fact that you have never been recognized as a world-class athlete is one thing, but to have Olympic officials ask your name in order to post it upon the victory board is quite another. Yet this is precisely what happened to the American distance-runner Billy Mills.

Of the restlessly stretching runners gathered at the start of the 10,000-meter race, only three, the Australian Ron Clarke among them, were given a chance to win the gold. In addition to possessing great physical gifts, Clarke was also a master strategist. Taking the lead at the beginning of the race, he picked up the pace every other lap, sapping the energy of those who tried to keep up. At the 5,000-meter mark this tactic had apparently worked on those who had the best chances to challenge Clarke for the win. But near the end of the race, two runners, Mohamed Gammoudi of Tunisia and Billy Mills, were still right behind the Australian.

Unfortunately for Clarke, as he neared the finish line he ran into a traffic jam of lapped runners. Clarke swerved left and shoved Mills, who stumbled and almost fell. This gave Gammoudi his chance. Jamming his way like a full-back between the two leaders, he pushed both aside and took the lead. Clarke sprinted after Gammoudi, with Mills just behind him. But Mills felt great: "I knew at that stage that I was the fastest man on the track," he said. This was certainly true as he passed Clarke and then Gammoudi to win by 0.4 second.

Who is this guy? everyone asked. Part Native American, Billy Mills was a man whose previous best showing in the 10,000 was 46 seconds slower than the time he had just run to win the Olympic gold medal.

191

Left and right: American Don Schollander, winner of four gold medals in swimming

SWIMMING RECORDS

The Tokyo games witnessed significant turning points in Olympic swimming history. Whereas in earlier games a few stars tended to win multiple medals, in 1964—with the exception of the American freestyler Don Schollander, who won four gold medals—there were no real standouts.

At the same time, what is so remarkable about the 1964 Olympic swimming meet was that either a world or an Olympic record was set in every single one of the nineteen men's and women's finals. True, several previous gold medalists had returned to compete, but for the most part, 1964 was a career year for the Tokyo champions, establishing a trend that would hold in subsequent years.

Despite the absence of dominant multiple winners, Olympic swimming had become an international favorite, especially on television. After the Tokyo games, perhaps partially in response to the public enthusiasm for the sport, the number of events almost doubled.

Between the 1964 Tokyo games and the 1968 Mexico City games, men's swimming contests grew from eight to thirteen. Existing events were supplemented with the 200-meter freestyle, the 100-meter breaststroke, the 100-meter backstroke, the 100-meter butterfly and the 200-meter individual medley. The growth of the women's swim meet was even more spectacular, from seven events held in 1964 to thirteen in 1968. (Added were the 200- and 800-meter freestyle, the 200-meter backstroke, the 100-meter breaststroke, the 200-meter butterfly and the 200-meter individual medley.)

1964 SWIMMING: A RECORD IN EVERY EVENT

MEN'S RESULTS					WOMEN'S RESULTS				
100m Freestyle	D. Schollander	USA	53.4	OR	100m Freestyle	D. Fraser	AUS	59.5	OR
400m Freestyle	D. Schollander	USA	4:12.2	WR	400m Freestyle	V. Duenkel	USA	4:43.3	OR
1,500m Freestyle	R. Windle	AUS	17:01.7	OR	100m Backstroke	C. Ferguson	USA	1:07.7	WR
200m Backstroke	J. Graef	USA	2:10.3	WR	200m Breaststroke	G. Prozumenshikova	SOV	2:46.4	OR
200m Breaststroke	I. O'Brien	AUS	2:27.8	WR	100m Butterfly	S. Stouder	USA	1:04.7	WR
200m Butterfly	K. Berry	AUS	2:06.6	WR	400m Ind Medley	D. de Varona	USA	5:18.7	OR
400m Ind Medley	R. Roth	USA	4:45.4	WR					

OR = Olympic Record   WR = World Record

193

Bob Hayes (USA), first to run Olympic 100 meters in 10 seconds, wins heat

BOB HAYES

One of the benefits accrued by the winner of the Olympic 100-meter sprint has traditionally been his widely acknowledged though certainly unofficial designation as the "world's fastest human." In 1964, this appellation was the subject of practically no dispute. Prior to the games, the Florida A & M University sprinter Bob Hayes had run the 100-yard dash in 9.1 seconds and the 60-yard race in 6.0 seconds, both world-record times. In the final at the Tokyo games, he steadily distanced himself from the rest of the pack and won by a phenomenal 2 meters, equalling the world record in the event.

How would Hayes have fared against the fifteen previous Olympic "world's fastest humans"? Obviously that is an impossible question to answer. Simply taking into account the variables of track conditions and training methods renders any comparison between runners wildly speculative.

But it is interesting to look at the Olympic 100-meter results in the modern era and see the progressive pattern of improving times. Discounting Thomas Burke's initial 12.0-second record at the 1896 Athens games, winning times seem to bunch together in groups. From 1900 to 1906, approximately 11 seconds seemed to be the standard winning time. For the next twenty years (1908 to 1928) about 0.2 second was lopped off the typical gold medalist's time. Then, discounting Bobby Morrow's 10.5-second time in 1956, there was a thirty-year period when a 10.2- or 10.3-second time was needed to gain victory. Finally, with Hayes's winning time of 10.0, a new era, it appeared, had begun.

194

Peter Snell (NZE; 466) passes to win 1,500. Following pages: Spectators in rainy Olympic stadium.

MEN'S TRACK: 100-METER GOLD-MEDAL PERFORMANCES

Year	Athlete	Country	Time		Year	Athlete	Country	Time
1896	T. Burke	USA	12.0 seconds		1952	L. Remingino	USA	10.4
1900	F. Jarvis	USA	11.0		1956	B. Morrow	USA	10.5
1904	A. Hahn	USA	11.0		1960	A. Hary	GER	10.2
1906	A. Hahn	USA	11.2		1964	B. Hayes	USA	10.0
1908	R. Walker	SAF	10.8		1968	J. Hines	USA	9.95
1912	R. Craig	USA	10.8		1972	V. Borzov	URS	10.14
1920	C. Paddock	USA	10.8		1976	H. Crawford	TRI	10.06
1924	H. Abrahams	GBR	10.6		1980	A. Wells	GBR	10.25
1928	P. Williams	CAN	10.8		1984	C. Lewis	USA	9.99
1932	E. Tolan	USA	10.3		1988	C. Lewis	USA	9.92
1936	J. Owens	USA	10.3		1992	L. Christie	GBR	9.96
1948	H. Dillard	USA	10.3					

American 200-meter gold and bronze medalists Tommie Smith and John Carlos raise Black Power salute

Mexico City
1968

All-around gymnastics champion Vera Caslavska (CZE)

As a rule, in the period leading up to the start of a new set of games, Olympic athletes care not a whit about politics. Conditions, conditioning and the quality of the competition are what troubles them, not the worrisome affairs of the world around them. As the 1968 Mexico City Olympics approached, however, hovering in the air over the games were two very different sorts of problems. The first of these was political; the second was geographical.

Though the Mexicans had recently constructed a beautiful new stadium and though the number of nations sending athletes had risen to an all-time high of 112, there was a major problem with the site. Mexico City sits 7,573 feet above sea level, which is more than 7,000 feet higher than the altitude of any previous Olympic venue. It was thought that the thin air would cause all sorts of physical problems for the athletes, particularly for those competing in events that demanded endurance. This it did, with one interesting proviso: Athletes who lived or trained in countries where conditions resembled those of Mexico City seemed to have an edge over their opponents.

Take the 10,000-meter run, for instance. As the race neared its end, the thin air began to claim casualties. Several runners collapsed and were carried off. The race came down to four athletes from high-altitude countries: Naftali Temu of Kenya, Mamo Wolde of Ethiopia, Mohamed Gammoudi of Tunisia and the Mexican runner Juan Martinez. After a back-and-forth battle, Temu narrowly won, ahead of Wolde, Gammoudi and Martinez, in that order.

Another Kenyan runner, Kip Keino, defeated the American Jim Ryun, the world-record holder in the demanding 1,500-meter race. True, both men had physical problems: Ryun was recovering from mononucleosis and Keino was

Team-pursuit cycling race, decided when third member of fastest team crosses line

suffering from a gall-bladder infection. Keino ran a smart race, however, getting so far out front that Ryun's famous kick would have had to be superhuman to allow him to catch up. A similar mixture of conditions and strategy almost certainly influenced the 3,000-meter steeplechase. During the final heat yet another Kenyan, Amos Biwott, won by an unusually large margin, despite the fact that his technique, at least in the eyes of the traditional steeplechasers, was terrible. As one observer noted, "He cleared the hurdles like he feared they had spikes embedded on the top."

The thin air apparently favored other track-and-field athletes, though in at least one of these events, altitude mixed unexpectedly with the other great issue of the games: the political climate. The battle in the 200-meter sprint was, as expected, waged by two Americans, Tommie Smith and John Carlos, both of San Jose State. Smith won in world-record time, with Carlos coming in a close third behind the Australian Peter Norman. But when they mounted the victory stand, the two American athletes raised black-gloved fists in a defiant gesture of solidarity with the civil-rights struggle being waged in the United States. Both runners were suspended by the U.S. Olympic Committee.

Most of the athletes were more concerned about competition than about controversy. "The black-gloved salute didn't bother me all that much," pole-vaulter Bob Seagren has said. "I had traveled all over the world with Tommie Smith and John Carlos and I knew them as individuals." In fact, even though the final round of the vaulting was briefly delayed by the incident, it seemed to have no effect on the outcome of the competition, which Seagren won on the basis of fewer misses.

Kip Keino (KEN) breaks 1,500-meter world record of Jim Ryun (USA; 285)

Indeed, most of the athletes competing in Mexico City simply went about their business. The American Wyomia Tyus again secured her status as the world's fastest female in winning the 100-meter sprint; she additionally anchored the last leg of the winning 4 X 100-meter relay race. And Lia Manoliu of Romania, who had competed in four previous games, won the discus, setting an Olympic record in the process.

Five new events were added to the women's swimming schedule: the 200- and 800-meter freestyle, the 100-meter breaststroke, the 200-meter butterfly and the 400-meter individual medley. In a sense, this was as revolutionary as any of the more hotly debated political incidents. For the first time, women were considered equal to men in their ability to tackle a variety of swimming styles and distances. Accordingly, these new events produced new champions, most noticeably the American Debbie Meyer, who by winning the 200-, 400- and 800-meter races became the first swimmer, male or female, to win three individual golds in a single games.

In another departure from the norm, India lost the field-hockey championship for the first time in twenty-eight years. And for the second time in a row, a future professional heavyweight champion, George Foreman, took the super-heavyweight title. The incident most typical of standard Olympic controversy, however, took place after the middleweight boxing final. The winner, Chris Finnegan, was asked to take a routine drug test, but he couldn't, explaining candidly that standing "at those long urinals . . . with all the other blokes" made him terribly uneasy. Not until many hours later did Finnegan win the final bout, certifying his Olympic gold-medalist status.

Beamon breaks teammate Ralph Boston's world record and collapses afterward, comforted by Boston

BOB BEAMON

In 1968 Bob Beamon was by all accounts the most talented long jumper in the world. In the year or so leading up to the games he had lost only once. But Beamon was an emotional, unorthodox, sometimes mercurial competitor who, after a disagreement with his University of Texas coach about the racial policies of Brigham Young University, had been suspended from his college track team.

During the qualifying round, Beamon was so jittery that he fouled twice and risked disqualification. At this point, his friend Ralph Boston, the 1960 champion, reminded Beamon that in 1936, Jesse Owens had also found himself one foul away from disqualification. Boston suggested that Beamon follow the advice given to Owens by a German competitor and set his take-off mark well behind the official line. Beamon did so and qualified comfortably.

On his first jump of the finals, Beamon composed himself, sprinted down the runway, and after a perfect take-off propelled his body upward and outward in a trajectory that has been estimated to be almost 6-feet high at its peak. All watching knew that this was an incredible jump. Track officials quickly moved their electronic eye to measure the leap, but Beamon's mark outdistanced the machine's capabilities. A tape measure was brought out, and the officials read the numbers: 8.9 meters, or 29' 2½", nearly 2 feet longer than the world record.

Beamon's emotions were not as yet completely under control, however. After the distance was displayed on the results board, Beamon collapsed, overcome by what his doctors later described as "an atonic state of the somatic muscles which develops suddenly on the heels of emotional excitement."

At thirty-two, Al Oerter (USA) wins fourth straight Olympic discus championship

AL OERTER

In Mexico City Al Oerter, competing in his fourth consecutive games, was probably as healthy as he had been in the last eight or ten years. A year after he had won his first gold medal in the discus, at the Melbourne Olympics, Oerter was in a terrible automobile accident and it appeared that his career might be over. But Oerter always viewed training as a "recreation," and after much hard work he was ready to compete in Rome. That year his principal rival was his American teammate Richard "Rink" Babka, whose first throw in the final was a foot longer than Oerter's best. Oerter's final throw, however, was his longest of the day and he ended up beating Babka by nearly 4 feet.

Shortly before the Tokyo games, his third, Oerter was again in bad physical shape. A cervical disc injury had flared up and he had also torn rib cartilage. Taped, iced and medicated with novocaine, he told a friend, "If I don't do it on the first throw, I won't be able to do it at all." But with his back facing the throwing circle, a technique he had invented, he became "inspired," and his extremely painful final toss went 200' 1", setting a new Olympic record and outdistancing his closest competitor's best effort by about a foot and a half.

In 1968 Oerter, at thirty-two, was the old man of the discus event. The field was strong. Oerter's teammate Jay Silvester was the world-record holder and several other throwers were given a good chance to win the gold. But Oerter did it once again. In the third round he hurled the discus 212' 11", his all-time personal best. Having won his fourth consecutive gold medal, Oerter retired. In 1980, however, he tried out for the Olympic team again and finished fourth, almost qualifying at the age of forty-four.

Dick Fosbury begins backward upside-down leap (left), following through with his signature Fosbury Flop (right)

THE FOSBURY FLOP

The basic scientific rule at work in the high jump is simply stated: The lower the jumper's center of gravity, the greater the possibility that he or she will make a winning leap. Though it is doubtful that many high jumpers in Olympic history have reflected on the physical laws governing their athletic art, the stylistic changes made by Olympic high jumpers over the years have clearly, if unknowingly, been predicated upon this scientific axiom.

Early Olympic high jumpers utilized the scissors style, jumping upward while their bodies remained vertical to the bar. This method resembled a sort of side-step fence-leap. The principal drawback of this technique is the body's very high center of gravity. At the 1912 games George Horine introduced the western-roll style of jumping, in which the jumper passed over the bar on his side with his knees tucked together. Despite the scientific superiority of the western roll, Horine came in third behind the scissors-kicking Alma Richards.

The next notable improvement in high-jumping technique was the introduction of the straddle-style leap, in which the jumper's leading arm and leg passed over the bar with the rest of his body, facedown, following. This was an extremely efficient technique that enabled the American high-jumper Charlie Dumas to be the first athlete to break the 7-foot barrier.

In Mexico City this was all changed by the American Dick Fosbury, who ran toward the bar in a semi-circular direction and leaped headfirst and upside down. This way, it is said, the jumper's center of gravity actually passes under the bar. Despite its oddity, this new style, called the Fosbury Flop, earned its namesake an Olympic gold.

Following pages: In the 200 meters, American Tommie Smith defeats teammate John Carlos by .04 second

THE EVOLUTION OF THE HIGH JUMP

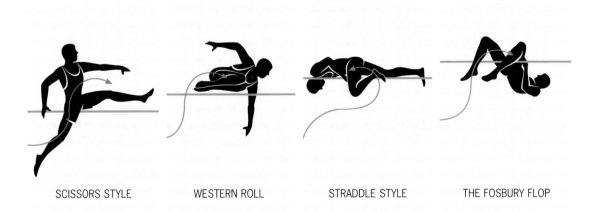

SCISSORS STYLE   WESTERN ROLL   STRADDLE STYLE   THE FOSBURY FLOP

Closing ceremonies of 1972 Olympic Games

Munich
1972

Frank Shorter (USA), winner of the 1972 marathon

All host nations work diligently to make their edition of the Olympic Games the most beautifully situated, the most accommodating and the best organized to date. This was the German Olympic Committee's goal, but in addition it also clearly felt it had the duty to repay a lingering historical debt. The last time the games had been held in Germany, Adolf Hitler had attempted to fashion them into a political advertisement. This would not happen in the new Germany, Olympic officials pledged, but political events seldom fall under the control of Olympic officials and Munich would come to be known for the single most horrifying event in the history of the games.

By and large the Munich games were extraordinarily well run. The Olympic village was hospitable and friendly. The communications center was so well designed that when the thousands of athletes from 122 nations marched into the stadium on opening day, the ceremony was watched by over one billion people worldwide.

From the first day of finals to the last, the athletic drama was intense. On Tuesday, August 28, the American swimmer Mark Spitz won his first two finals: the 200-meter butterfly and the 4 X 100-meter relay. In one day he had equalled his 1968 gold-medal performances.

Swimming action continued the next day. Spitz again won, this time in the 200-meter freestyle, a victory he celebrated exuberantly. Two other of the meet's most talented athletes also swam that day. The Australian women's swimming champion Shane Gould could manage only third place in the 100-meter freestyle, but the great German backstroker Roland Matthes repeated his 1968 performance by winning the men's 100-meter race. Gould returned

209

Soviet Olga Korbut in winning floor-exercise program

to the pool the next day to take the 400-meter freestyle, breaking the world-record time by almost 3 seconds.

But that day—Thursday, August 30—the attention of viewers all over the world shifted to the Olympic arena, where Sawal Kato, the 5' 3" Japanese gymnast, won his second gold medal in a row in the men's all-around competition, the second man ever to repeat. In women's gymnastics the competition was perhaps more fierce. Soviet Lyudmila Tourishcheva took the all-around title only after her teammate—the crowd's favorite, the 4' 11" seventeen-year-old Olga Korbut—fell off the uneven parallel bars and was given a score so low that it became impossible for her to remain in contention.

On Friday morning, Korbut returned to compete in the individual events, winning two and finishing second in one. All that day attention had been shifting back and forth from the arena to the pool, where Spitz once again garnered double victories: first in the 100-meter butterfly and an hour later in the 4 X 200-meter freestyle relay. Spitz now was the possessor of five gold medals and five world records. Back at the arena, now emptied of gymnastic equipment, the Soviet wrestler Aleksandr Medved was engaged in his first-round bout with the huge 6' 5", 412-pound American Chris Taylor, a match that ended with Taylor's controversial disqualification for passivity.

Saturday was a day for both swimming and track-and-field. Shane Gould, by this time over her initial loss, easily beat world-record-holder Shirley Babashoff in the 200-meter freestyle to win her second gold. That same day, the American winner of the men's 400 meters, Rick DeMont, was disqualified and forced to return his medal after it was

discovered that he had been using a banned asthma medicine. There was also a problem on the track that day. Two American sprinters, Eddie Hart and Rey Robinson, misread the 100-meter heat schedule and arrived too late to compete. Whatever their disappointments, there was no controversy about the final, which the Soviet Valery Borzov won going away.

The real excitement on Sunday was also on the track. Though he had earlier that year equalled the world record in the 800 meters, the American Dave Wottle was not given much chance to win in Munich, a prediction that seemed reliable most of the way through the race. Rounding the last curve, Wottle was running in sixth place when he saw his chance. Wearing his trademark golf cap, he sprinted past the four lead runners and crossed the finish line just inches ahead of the favorite, the Soviet Yevgeny Arzhanov.

The next two days were relatively quiet, distinguished mainly by Spitz's sixth and seventh wins, in the 100-meter freestyle and the 4 X 100-meter medley relay, for which he swam the butterfly leg. Borzov also returned to the track, double-medaling by winning the 200-meter sprint. About the same time another Soviet, the reigning Olympic triple-jump champion Viktor Saneyev, narrowly defeated the German Jorg Drehmel to win the second of his three consecutive gold medals in that event.

Then it happened. In the predawn hours of Wednesday morning, Palestinian terrorists broke into the quarters of the Israeli Olympic team, killing the wrestling coach and a weightlifter and taking nine athletes hostage. Police

211

American basketball players celebrate apparent victory over Soviet Union

surrounded the compound. A standoff began and later that day all athletic events were officially suspended. That evening, during a botched rescue attempt, the terrorists shot and killed all their hostages and were subsequently killed by police.

It was not until two days later, after a Thursday morning memorial service, that competition resumed, though even then the intense and excited mood of the games remained severely dampened. After their first and second places in the 400-meter race, the Americans Vincent Matthews and Wayne Collett appeared to fidget on the victory stand; Olympic officials, perhaps fearing a reprise of the 1968 victory-stand incident, accused the two of disrespect while their national anthem was playing and permanently banned them from further competition.

Saturday, fortunately, was a relatively untroubled day, notable chiefly for the initial running of the women's 1,500-meter race, which was won by the Soviet Lyudmila Bragina. Sunday, September 10, was the last day of the games. Two American archers, John Williams and Doreen Wilbur, won the individual titles, the first medals given in archery since the event had been discontinued in 1908. And the Cuban Teofilo Stevenson won the first of his unprecedented three successive heavyweight boxing titles.

To end the athletically exciting but emotionally exhausting Olympics, the American Frank Shorter jogged into the stadium to win the marathon, but only to be met by jeers. The heckling was directed not at him, as he had thought, but at an imposter who only seconds earlier had been dragged off the track by security guards.

212

BASKETBALL

Basketball as an Olympic event had been introduced in 1936 at the Berlin Olympics. Knowing little about the sport, the organizers of the competition held the games outdoors on a clay tennis court, which after a night of heavy rain turned the finals into something resembling basketball on ice.

In the years between 1936 and 1972, the United States, where the game had been invented, did not lose a single one of the sixty-two games it played. Indeed, as American professional basketball began to gain in popularity, many of the collegians competing in the Olympics—including K. C. Jones, Bill Russell, Oscar Robertson, Jerry West and Bill Bradley—went on to become well-known professional stars.

The 1972 team, though perhaps as not well stocked with future legends as some, was made up of extremely talented players, and seemed on its way to an eighth straight gold medal. But the Soviet Union had put a lot of time and money into its basketball team, which was for the first time competitive with the Americans.

The tournament final round between the Soviets and the Americans was a tight, exciting contest. The U.S.S.R. led for most of the game, but with 6 seconds left and his team trailing by one point, American Doug Collins sank two free throws to put the U.S. ahead 50–49. With 2 seconds left on the clock, the ruckus began. The Soviet coach was found to have called time immediately after Collins's last shot. But then, unaccountably, the clock was reset to 3 seconds. The Soviets inbounded the ball and passed the length of the court to Sasha Belov, who drove past the stunned Americans to score the winning basket.

213

MONTREAL 1976 MONTREAL 1976 MONTREAL 1976 **Opening ceremonies of Montreal games** MONTREAL 1976 MONTREAL 1976 MONTREAL 1976

Montreal
1976

400-meter champion Alberto Juantorena wins 800 meters

In 1976, the memory of Munich was crowded not with heats, finals and the playings of national anthems, but was instead a single memory of one hooded man, a rifle hanging at his side, peering over the balcony of a plain concrete building in the Olympic village. This powerful image was apparently preeminent in the minds of the organizers of the 1976 games, for the athletes arrived to discover the Montreal Olympic sites overrun by sixteen thousand armed police and soldiers, who in an effort to provide security tracked every move of all in attendance.

The main political problem, however, at least as it concerned athletics, was a large-scale boycott. In 1974, a New Zealand rugby team had traveled to South Africa, still banned from Olympic competition due to its racial policies. When the International Olympic Committee refused to bar New Zealand from the 1976 games, twenty-two African nations recalled their athletes from Montreal.

Consequently, a number of very talented athletes were missing from events in which they would have unquestionably raised the level of competition. This was primarily true of the longer distance races. This is not to say that these fields were weak. There were, for instance, many fine runners in the 1,500-meter race, but missing were the world-record-holder, Tanzanian Filbert Bayi, and the equally gifted Kenyan Mike Boit. Without the Africans it was a slow race, with New Zealander John Walker's winning time almost 7 seconds off Bayi's world record.

Though Africans had won three out of the past four marathons, the 1976 event was nonetheless a terrific race. The American Frank Shorter was well in the lead when an unranked East German steeplechaser, Waldemar

217

Left: John Walker (NZE) coasts to 1,500-meter victory

Cierpinski, decided that the pace was too slow and caught up with the leader. Well before the entry to the stadium Cierpinski sprinted past Shorter and began his solo run-in.

The boycott had less effect on the middle-distance races. The great Cuban Alberto Juantorena was favored to win both the 400 and the 800 meters, which he did, becoming, after the 1906 victor Paul Pilgrim, only the second man to double in these events.

Canadian officials had done a relatively poor job with the construction of its facilities, which some athletes publicly criticized. The American high-jumper Dwight Stones was loudly booed after he complained that with the stadium's retractable roof unfinished, he in particular would have trouble getting his footing on the wet ground.

The somewhat lopsided results of the swimming contests also had a distinctly nationalistic tone. The American men were on the whole still the strongest swimmers in the world. In Montreal Americans won twelve of the thirteen Olympic races, with John Naber winning one silver and four gold medals and his teammate Brian Goodell doubling in the 400- and 1,500-meter freestyle races.

And then there were the East German women, who had become so dominant that they were routinely accused of taking performance-enhancing drugs. Led by Kornelia Ender, swimmers from the German Democratic Republic came in just behind the American men, winning eleven of the thirteen swimming events. (The East German track-and-field female squad was only slightly less successful, winning nine of fourteen competitions.)

Center: Decathlon champion Bruce Jenner (USA). Right: Triple-jumper Viktor Saneyev (SOV).

    Not all, of course, was couched in the language of nation-against-nation rivalry. The ever-steady and seemingly invincible Cuban super-heavyweight boxer Teofilo Stevenson captured the second of his three gold medals, as did the practically unbeatable Soviet triple-jumper Viktor Saneyev. The 324-pound Soviet weightlifter Vasily Alexeyev, sometimes called the strongest man who ever lived, also easily won the super-heavyweight title, returning after the games to his home, where he cultivated fruits and vegetables and practiced his Tom Jones imitations when he was not training or competing.

    The Montreal games had displays of both good and bad sportsmanship. The modern pentathlon is one of the most demanding of Olympic events. A five-part contest, it is based on a simple military narrative: A soldier is sent on horseback to deliver a message. He stops to fight a duel with his sword. Winning this fight, he draws his pistol to shoot his way out of an ambush. He then swims across a river and runs the last 4,000 meters and hands over his message. In 1976, unfortunately, one of the pentathletes, the Soviet Boris Onischencko, decided to give himself an advantage by rigging his epee with a special button that allowed him to register touchés at will. He was disqualified.

    In shooting, however, there occurred a rare act of consummate sportsmanlike conduct. The small-bore rifle three-position match, which ended in a tie, was decided by a technicality that so annoyed the winner, Lanny Bassham, that during the medal ceremony he pulled silver-medalist Margaret Murdock, the first woman ever to make the team, up to the top step of the victory stand to share his moment of glory.

Lasse Viren (FIN) narrowly wins 5,000 meters

LASSE VIREN

The worst accusation directed at the great Finnish runners of the past had been that they were superhuman. Not so Lasse Viren, the inheritor of that brilliant long-distance running tradition. After winning two 1972 races, Viren was questioned by Olympic officials in Montreal about blood doping, a procedure by which a portion of an athlete's blood is extracted, stored and reinjected to increase the runner's oxygen-carrying capacity. Viren denied the charge, as did fellow competitor Frank Shorter, who said the truth was that "[Viren] was simply the best man in his field."

Viren's Olympic career began dramatically in Munich during the 10,000-meter race. With Viren in fifth place, he tripped over his own feet and fell down. Just behind him was the Tunisian Mohamed Gammoudi who, unable to avoid the fallen Viren, also came down heavily, so hard that he soon dropped out of the race. Viren, however, not only got up but sprinted ahead, caught the leaders, and on the last straightaway pulled away from the pack and coasted to a world record. Viren's win ten days later in the 5,000 was convincing if undramatic.

The same was true four years later when Viren won his second 10,000-meter race by almost 30 meters. The Montreal 5,000, however, was a closer and, for the Finn, a much more worrisome contest. Throughout most of the race Viren either led or shared the lead, in the process setting a sometimes murderous pace. At the start of the bell lap six runners were still keeping up with him. Viren was particularly haunted by Dick Quax of New Zealand, who was wearing a black uniform. But Viren found his self-described "last gear" and took off: "The black shadow glided away from my eyes. The holy sanctuary of the finish line engulfed me—I had won."

Kornelia Ender (GDR; left), winner over Shirley Babashoff (USA; right) in 200-meter freestyle

KORNELIA ENDER

A few years before the Montreal games, the East German women's swimming team seemed to appear out of nowhere to begin winning practically every single event in which they entered. Other swimmers could not help but notice the thick arms, shoulders and backs of the East German women, and thought they detected a suspicious team-wide trait: low, masculine speaking voices. Steroids, they thought—there could be no other explanation.

The star of the German team, Kornelia Ender, was big—5' 11", 170 pounds—and she in particular bore the brunt of the jokes. But Ender was a great swimmer. She had trained diligently, almost brutally, since a very young age, and her success was explained by German coaches as the product of a relentless schedule of hard work. By the time she arrived in Montreal, the seventeen-year-old Ender was nothing short of amazing. She won every event she entered, equalling or setting a world record in each. These triumphs only intensified the steroid allegations.

Fifteen years later, the truth came out: The swimmers had, unknown to them, been regularly given anabolic steroids. Though her accusers felt vindicated, Ender was horrified and embarrassed. As she said, "Medical men are the guilty people. They gave us things . . . to help us regenerate, we were never asked if we wanted it; it was just given." But were steroids the entire explanation for the successes of Ender and her teammates? True, Ender broke records by between one and two seconds. But if one looks at the men's competition in 1976, many records were broken by similar margins by Americans unaccused of drug abuse. Perhaps it was not just steroids, but also talent and training that affected the outcome of Ender's races.

Left and right: All-around gymnastics champion Nadia Comaneci (ROM)

NADIA COMANECI

They couldn't quite have passed for sisters—one was stockier with a rounder, more animated face, the other rail thin and impassive—but the two 4' 11" gymnasts shared the distinction of being the virtual creators of contemporary women's gymnastics.

Olympic women's gymnastics had never before been solely the province of very young, very diminutive athletes. The battle for the all-around title in 1956 was waged between thirty-five-year-old Agnes Keleti of Hungary and twenty-one-year-old Larissa Latynina of the Soviet Union, and was won by the younger woman only because Keleti scored poorly in a single event, the vault. Latynina continued to compete for the next eight years, taking first in 1960 and second in 1964.

The all-around winner in Tokyo, Vera Caslavska of Czechoslovakia, was young by her contemporary standards, having just turned twenty-two in 1964, but 1972 was the watershed year for age. Lyudmila Tourishcheva of the Soviet Union became, at nineteen, the youngest all-around gymnastics champion in Olympic history. But in a very real sense she was only paving the way for a couple of young, enormously gifted gymnasts who would represent the future of the sport.

The first of the two young girls was the Soviet Olga Korbut who, though she placed only seventh in the all-around in the 1972 games, so captivated the public that she became the first truly world-famous female gymnast. Korbut was clearly not as talented a member of her team as either the Munich gold-medalist Lyudmila Tourishcheva

222

Following pages: Comaneci with teammates. Backstroke gold-medalist John Naber (USA).

or even the young star Nelli Kim, but when Korbut returned to compete in 1976, it was she whom spectators were most anxious to see perform. Korbut was as charming as ever, if not quite as successful; she did rise to fifth place in the all-around but did not repeat her gold-medal victories in the floor exercises and the balance beam. The latter event was won—as was the all-around championship—by the other small, young, gifted female gymnast and crowd favorite, the Romanian Nadia Comaneci.

Comaneci was a quiet fourteen-year-old girl, shy and untalkative. When asked about receiving an unprecedented seven perfect scores on the uneven bars and the balance beam, she simply nodded and answered that the performances were perfect and were deserving of the judge's decisions.

But Comaneci, though by now world renowned, was not happy. A year after returning home, she tried to commit suicide. After being released from the hospital, she commented that at least she got out of training for a couple of days. Comaneci was pushed to continue her gymnastics career, however, and again won the balance beam and the floor exercises at the Moscow Olympics in 1980, but failed to repeat her victory in the all-around.

For the next few years Comaneci lived a luxurious and celebrated—if restrictive—life in Bucharest, personally looked after by Romanian dictator Nicolae Ceausescu. Late in 1989 Comaneci, then twenty-seven years old, escaped to the West, where thousands of young girls, inspired by her Olympic performances, were in training to become the next Nadia Comaneci.

Opening ceremonies in Moscow Olympic stadium

Moscow
1980

1980 MOSCOW 1980 MOSCOW   Aleksandr Dityatin (SOV) takes first in rings, one of 8 medals awarded to him in 1980   1980 MOSCOW 1980 MOSCOW

The Olympic Games were envisioned as an international event, open to any athlete from any country whatever his or her political persuasion. As the Turkish wrestler Mustafa Dagistanli once expressed it: "The Olympics is so beautiful, so big-hearted, so open to everything on the earth."

Of course, such a description is dreamily apolitical. Forget world affairs, this vision asks, and in doing so make the grandest, most symbolic affirmation of international peace and cooperation imaginable. Amazingly enough, for the most part the athletes themselves had no trouble with this concept. They were there, as Dagistanli said, to compete and, if possible, to win. Unfortunately this ambition was often not understood by leaders of nations, those non-athletes who competed on very different fields of play.

Shortly before the 1980 Moscow games were to begin, the Soviet Union invaded Afghanistan. The American government protested, to no avail. American politicians determined that there was no better way to punish the U.S.S.R. than to boycott the Olympic Games that Moscow had so eagerly petitioned to host, which is precisely what the United States Olympic Committee did, along with more than sixty nations that allied themselves with this symbolic gesture.

All this had minimal—if any—effect on the war in Afghanistan. The boycotts did, however, logically and inevitably alter the quality of athletic competition. For one thing, only eighty-one nations participated, representing a significant reduction, down forty countries from the all-time attendance at Munich. The international distribution of

Left: Miruts Yifter (ETH) captures 10,000 meters. Right: Shot-put silver-medalist Udo Beyer (GDR).

medals was severely curtailed by the reduction in the variety of athletes available to compete in any particular event, an inevitable consequence.

This is not to say that events at Moscow were unexciting. Athletic competition, whatever the circumstances, cannot fail to be dramatic. Daley Thompson of Great Britain, for instance, had been looking forward to an Olympic decathlon duel with his premier rival, Guido Kratschmer of West Germany. But unlike Britain, which honored the boycott but gave its athletes the option to compete, Germany had forbidden its athletes to attend. Even without serious competition, however, Thompson proceeded to equal the world record in Moscow.

The African nations, so noticeably absent in the long-distance races four years earlier due to their own boycott, were once again in attendance. This meant that the 5,000- and 10,000-meter races were probably no less electric and exciting than they would have been with a full field of international runners. Both of these races were won in the last laps when the Ethiopian Miruts Yifter, after fighting his way through traffic, shot ahead and outdistanced the field with his famous kick.

Unfortunately for the athletes, some of the events were overshadowed by a pall of outrageous officiating and equally awful behavior on the part of the Soviet spectators. Soviet officials in the track-and-field competition were responsible for several remarkable, indeed almost unprecedented, incidents: In the javelin competition, the Soviets opened the doors of the stadium to give their hurler the benefit of the wind, and on one occasion they deliberately

Left: Italian shot-putter Genovate Kjudite. Right: Tatyana Kazankina (URS) wins 1,500 meters.

mismeasured a Cuban discus thrower's best hurl in order to deprive him of a gold medal.

In addition to the biased judging, the spectators behaved badly throughout the games. In many cases, the audience reserved its boos and whistles for those athletes in attendance from the West. During the triple jump, for instance, the Soviets raised an unbelievable racket whenever the great Brazilian jumper Joao Carlos de Oliveira readied himself to compete against his Soviet competitors, Jaak Uudmae and Viktor Saneyev. (In this attempt to deprive de Oliveira of victory, the Soviets were also assisted by Soviet officials, who consistently called fouls against the Brazilian jumper.)

But it was not only Westerners who were objects of the crowd's derision and boorish behavior. As the East German discus-thrower Wolfgang Schmidt remembered: "I stepped into the ring for my first throw, and all of a sudden I heard spectators whistling. I was absolutely startled. My god, they had to mean me. Now *this* I could not fathom. I had thought of the Soviet Union as a brother country."

The East German women fared no better. In 1976, their track-and-field squad had been very powerful. In 1980, however, the Soviets, for whatever reason, won seven gold medals in women's track-and-field, while the East Germans dropped their total to five.

Despite all the cheating and disruptive catcalling, at least a few of the events rose to the normally high level of Olympic competition. In the women's long jump the field was extremely strong, and the lead bounced back and

Allan Wells of Great Britain (right), winner of 100-meter sprint

forth between the Soviets Tatiana Kolpakova and Tatiana Skachko, the East German Brigitte Wujak and the Pole Anna Wlodarczyk, with Kolpakova finally winning the gold medal by jumping 23' 2"—an impressive 9" farther than she had ever jumped before.

The gymnastics competition was also of established Olympic caliber. The men's all-around championship was won by the Soviet Aleksandr Dityatin who, in winning one bronze, four silver and three gold medals, became the first person to win eight medals in a single games. And though Nadia Comaneci was unable to repeat her 1976 victory in the all-around championship, her defeat came only in the last seconds of the meet. In order to win, Comaneci needed to score 9.9 on the balance beam, but she wavered ever so slightly and ended up losing to the Soviet Yelena Davydova by 0.75 point.

With athletes from the United States not in attendance, the swimming meets fell below world-class quality. The East German women were once again dominant, winning eleven of the scheduled thirteen events. And in men's swimming, the Soviet Union captured seven gold medals, a feat it had never even approached accomplishing in earlier Olympic Games.

In fact, though the Soviet Union had won the unofficial gold-medal race in four of the previous six games, in 1980 it won eighty first places, nearly double its usual number of such victories, making the Moscow games the Soviet games in more than name only.

COW 1980 MOSCOW 1980 Cuban boxer Teofilo Stevenson takes third successive gold medal in super-heavyweight division MOSCOW 1980 MOSCOW

TEOFILO STEVENSON

A number of Olympic boxing champions have gone on after the games to win professional world championships. But who was the greatest Olympic fighter of the modern Olympic era? That question will never be answered because the one man many thought might lay claim to that title refused to turn professional.

Teofilo Stevenson was, after Fidel Castro and Ché Guevara, the most famous name in Cuba. In Munich he quite simply annihilated his opponents, none of whom managed to last through an entire bout. The German heavyweight Peter Hussing, who stayed barely more than 4 minutes in the ring with Stevenson, said afterward, "I have never been hit so hard in all my 212 bouts. You just don't see his right hand. All of a sudden it is there—on your chin."

Boxing promoters practically surrounded Stevenson after the games, but he refused all offers, saying publicly, "Professional boxing treats a boxer like a commodity, to be bought, sold and discarded when he is no longer of use." Stevenson was if anything even more dominant at the 1976 games, winning his first three fights in about 7½ minutes. Stevenson's final bout was slightly longer, 2 rounds, but only due to the fact that before being disqualified the Romanian Mircea Simon spent the entire time quite assiduously running away from the Cuban.

In 1980, Stevenson once again won the Olympic heavyweight title. But Stevenson's effortless third consecutive Olympic victory bored boxing fans and, it appeared to some observers, wearied Stevenson himself. The Soviet Bloc boycott of the Los Angeles games ended the possibility that Stevenson would try for a fourth Olympic gold. He continued to refuse all offers to box professionally. "I have what I need," he said. "I feel happy inside."

Left: Ovett after 800-meter win. Center: Ovett (left), Steve Cram (GBR; middle) and Coe (right) in 1,500

SEBASTIAN COE AND STEVE OVETT

Olympic track-and-field rivalries are substantially different from those in other parts of the sporting world. Olympic track-and-field adversaries, though they wear national uniforms, are not so closely and keenly linked to a specific country as those participating in organized team sports such as soccer, baseball or even field hockey. True, a British fan may root for a British runner as will a Kenyan for a Kenyan, but for the most part, the emotional response does not really match the fervor displayed when a hometown team competes against that of a neighboring city.

Yet there is the fact that though international track-and-field athletes may have competed against each other dozens of times during the four years intervening between games, the outcome of none of these matches comes close to equalling the importance of capturing of an Olympic first place. One may be a world-record holder, a winner of almost every event he or she has entered, but the final validation of track-and-field success is the Olympic gold medal. Indeed, it is fair to say that such rivalries can only be truly settled in a single place: within the confines of an Olympic arena.

During the warm-up year leading into the 1980 games, only two men were seriously considered as probable victors of the 800-meter and 1,500-meter races—Great Britain's Sebastian Coe and Steve Ovett. Oddly enough, they had very rarely run against each other. Great Britain allowed its athletes to decide whether or not to compete in Moscow, and for these rivals, the choice was easy: Only an Olympic gold medal would truly certify which of the men was the fastest in the world at these distances.

232

Right: Coe after 1,500-meter victory. Following pages: Gymnastics exhibition on opening day.

Both were running as well as they ever had. Indeed, the two were breaking world records with rather astonishing regularity. In July 1979, Coe ran the 800 meters in 1:42.33, bettering the Cuban Alberto Juantorena's world-record time by one second. A month later, after also achieving a world record in the mile, Coe added the 1,500-meter record to his list. The following summer Ovett also began breaking records, lowering Coe's mile time by one tenth of a second and, a few days later, tying his rival's world record in the 1,500 meters. Prior to arriving in Moscow, most track-and-field pundits predicted that Coe, still the fastest at 800 meters, had the better chance to win that distance. Victory in the 1,500-meter race, it was thought, could go to either man. They were wrong.

The first of these races to be run in Moscow was the 800 meters, and for a while it looked as if neither of the two British runners were in contention. For a good deal of the race, Ovett was stuck in the pack in sixth place and Coe was running dead last. Ovett then began to surge ahead, jostling other runners and shoving his body forward. This tactic worked, and fewer than 100 meters from the finish line Ovett took the lead. Coe had meanwhile also begun to sprint, but by this time he had too much ground to cover and he barely managed to finish second to Ovett, the upset winner.

A few days later, however, it was Coe's turn. Though Jurgen Staub of East Germany led the 1,500 for most of the race, Coe overtook him in the last 200 meters for the win. Ovett, stuck behind Staub, came in a disappointing third.

233

ELES 1984 LOS ANGELES 1984 LOS ANGELES 1984 Opening ceremony of the Los Angeles games LOS ANGELES 1984 LOS ANGELES 1984 LOS A

Los Angeles
1984

West German Michael Gross, world-record setter in 200-meter freestyle and 100-meter butterfly

"Oh, what we've done to the Olympics," the sportswriter Frank Deford observed sadly after the Los Angeles games. Specifically, Deford was referring to the unavoidable, indeed omnipresent, crass commercialism and jingoism that arose like a Technicolor cartoon cloud above the third Olympic summer games to be hosted by the United States. Four years earlier in Moscow, the prevailing atmosphere had been perceived as full of gloom. Now it was as if American organizers, in their eagerness to do it right, had decided to produce the biggest, brightest, most appealing athletic spectacle ever seen in the history of sport, as if they were marketing a new movie.

To the rest of the world, however, especially to those watching courtesy of American television, it appeared that ninety cents of every dollar spent on the games went to flag waving, with only a dime saved for the splendor of international sports. The absence of athletes from the Soviet Union and thirteen of its allies, due to "security" reasons, made the Los Angeles games look like the flip side of those held in Moscow. In plain terms, the Olympic Games appeared, at first glance, to be patently one-sided: the American games.

Yet if one looks past the media coverage and concentrates on the games themselves, many events were as athletically exciting as they had always been. True, the absence of Eastern-bloc athletes sometimes diminished fields of competition, but not as unfavorably as it would seem. Take, for instance, the middle- and long-distance races, none of which was won by an American. Though Sebastian Coe of Great Britain had returned to avenge his loss in the 800 meters, it was a Brazilian, Joaquim Cruz, who took the gold. Cruz was also scheduled to run the 1,500-

Daley Thompson (GBR) equals his world record with second decathlon title

meter race but was forced to withdraw for health reasons, leaving Coe and his teammates Steve Cram and world-record-holder Steve Ovett as the favorites. Ovett, however, experienced chest pains and dropped out in the last lap, leaving Jose Abascal of Spain in the lead. Cram, now in third place, made the first move, pulling up on Coe, who sped up to pass Abascal and eventually crossed the finish line a tenth of a second ahead of his countryman.

Americans were also minor, if not inconsequential, players in the longer races. The 5,000-meter race, for example, which was won by Said Aouita of Morocco, was run in record time not only by the victor but also by the next four finishers, all of whom ran the fastest 5,000 meters of their lives. It was predicted that the 10,000-meter race would be a duel between Alberto Cova of Italy and world-record-holder Fernando Mamede of Portugal. Mamede, however, often suffered terrible anxiety attacks during big races. Partway through the competition, Mamede dropped out, leaving Cova to battle and finally defeat Marti Vainio of Finland during the last lap of the race. Vainio later tested positive for steroids and was disqualified.

National pride contributed to the rousing receptions showered upon the winners of the two walk races. A large number of Mexican-Americans lined the course to cheer the victors of both the 20,000- and 50,000-meter walks, both of whom represented Mexico. The crowd was just as enthusiastic, though perhaps not quite as nationalistic, as it cheered the victory of Portugal's Carlos Lopes in the marathon, who bested one of that event's strongest fields ever. There is no doubt, however, that the absence of the Soviet Bloc athletes affected many of the field events.

238

ANGELES 1984 LOS ANGELES 1984   All-around winner Mary Lou Retton (USA) scores 10s in floor and vault   LOS ANGELES 1984 LOS ANGELES 1984

Missed, in particular, were pole-vaulter Sergei Bubka, hammer throwers Yuri Sedykh and Sergei Litvinov and javelin-specialist Uwe Hohn. Yet the absence of these men from competition did not open the door to easy American victories. Indeed, America's only two gold medals in field events were awarded to Carl Lewis in the long jump and Al Joyner in the triple jump.

Neither did Americans win the majority of gold medals in women's track-and-field. True, some American women runners were splashy and spectacular. Evelyn Ashford took the 100-meter sprint, as did Valerie Brisco-Hooks the 200- and 400-meter races, and Joan Benoit won the women's marathon—the first one in Olympic history—by almost 2 minutes. But in the field events there was not a single American gold medalist.

Though it was certainly competitive and produced a number of world and Olympic records, the 1984 Olympic swimming meet was by contrast dominated by the Americans. Victor Davis of Canada won the 200-meter breast-stroke, his teammate Alex Bauman won both individual medleys and Jon Seiben of Australia took the gold medal in the 200-meter butterfly—and that was it for non-American gold medalists.

Americans also performed spectacularly well in women's swimming. As with the men's meet, only three non-Americans won their races. The Dutch swimmers Jolande de Rover and Petra van Steveren won the 200-meter back-stroke and the 100-meter breaststroke respectively, and Anne Ottenbrite of Canada took first in the 200-meter breaststroke. The American freestyler Tiffany Cohen doubled in the 400 and 800 meters as did Mary Meagher in

239

Left: Brazilian 800-meter winner Joaquim Cruz. Right: American cyclist Connie Carpenter.

the 100-meter and 200-meter butterfly races. Tracy Caulkins went her teammates one better by gold-medaling in three races: the 200- and 400-meter medleys and the 4 X 100-medley relay.

The lack of Eastern European competition also affected the gymnastics events, though it must be said that in terms of crowd appeal the close competition for the men's all-around title between Peter Vidmar and Koji Gushiken, as well as the brilliant performance of the short, muscular Mary Lou Retton probably made up for the fact that these were not truly international meets.

In at least one event, partisanship had nothing to do with an American victory. After losing to downhill-skier-turned-cyclist Steve Hegg in the 400-meter individual pursuit race, silver-medalist Rolf Golz said, "You wouldn't have beaten me in Germany." Hegg shot back, "I really don't care—this is Los Angeles." As it turned out, location probably had little to do with the results.

Certainly the fact that no Eastern-bloc wrestlers or weightlifters were in attendance in Los Angeles skewed the results of those events. No American had ever won a medal in Greco-Roman wrestling, but Jeff Blatnik defeated the favorite, Refik Memisevic of Yugoslavia, in the semifinal and went on to win the gold. The triumph was especially heroic as Blatnik had recently been treated for Hodgkin's Disease, the illness that had already killed his brother. In front of an international viewing-audience of millions, Blatnik knelt on the mat, raised his hands as if in prayer, and cried.

Taking exactly 13 steps between hurdles, Edwin Moses wins 400 meters

EDWIN MOSES

As a child, Edwin Moses was more interested in science and engineering than in sports. But as a freshman at Morehouse College in Atlanta, he made the track team as a 110-meter hurdler and as a 400-meter flat racer. He was not outstanding in either of these events.

At a track meet in the spring of 1976, Moses also entered the 400-meter hurdles and, despite the fact that Moses lost, the American Olympic track coach LeRoy Walker saw something in Moses that others had missed. Walker recounted, "His size and his speed, his base, his ability to carry his stride, his skim—what we call the measurement of the stride over the hurdle, he had it all." Moses, with some coaching, qualified for the 400-meter hurdles in the 1976 games. This, however, was the year of the African Olympic boycott, and though Moses won the gold medal in Montreal in world-record time, some grumbled that it would have been a better race had the previous world-record holder, John Aki Bua of Uganda, been able to run.

Moses missed the Moscow games due to the U.S. boycott, but in Los Angeles in 1984 he won his second Olympic gold, striding precisely thirteen times between hurdles, to win by nearly a full second. Still more remarkable was the fact that for almost ten years—from August 26, 1977, until June 4, 1987—Moses did not lose a single race. But Moses shook off even the June 4 defeat, saying with typical candor, "The streak was made concrete by the loss." Moses continued to run, finishing third in the 1988 Seoul games. Again he shook off the defeat. "The other guys just ran their best races," he explained, as if any explanation was necessary. "And I didn't."

241

Left: Mary Decker (USA) leaves track in tears. Center: Britain's Zola Budd (barefoot).

MARY DECKER, ZOLA BUDD AND JOAN BENOIT

If particular races can be said to have personalities of their own, no two could be more different than the 1984 women's 3,000-meter and marathon races, both held for the first time in the 1984 Olympics. The American Mary Decker was favored to win the 3,000. During the ten years leading up to the 1984 games, Decker had been the most sensational and controversial runner in the women's track world. Even at the age of twelve she was a phenomenon, competing in the 400-meter, 800-meter, one-mile, two-mile and marathon races all within the space of a week. But Decker's abilities often collided with her emotions. During a 4 x 800-meter relay race in Moscow she responded to a push by hurling her baton at the offending Soviet runner. In addition, Decker had begun to experience chronic pain while running and was eventually diagnosed with a muscle injury known as "Compartment Syndrome." After an operation to correct the problem, Decker returned to world-class form. In the summer of 1982 she was running so well that she set a world record in the mile, and in 1983 won the inaugural World Championships 1500- and 3,000-meter races.

The South African Zola Budd, running for Great Britain, was also slated for the 3,000. Like her hero Decker, Budd was a sensation. An eighteen-year-old South African who preferred to run barefoot, Budd had easily broken Decker's 5,000-meter world record in 1983. As Budd's country was still banned from Olympic competition, however, it seemed that there would be no Olympic duel between the two. Fortunately for Budd, her grandfather was a British citizen and arrangements were made for the young runner to settle in England and be awarded British

Right: Joan Benoit (USA) finishes marathon ahead of Grete Waitz (NOR)

citizenship. Though there were objections to this maneuver, prompting excoriation by some members of the press, Budd was allowed to travel to Los Angeles to compete in the inaugural Olympics women's 3,000-meter race.

Besides Decker and Budd, there were two other contenders in the race: Maricica Puica of Romania and Wendy Sly of Great Britain. At 1,700 meters, the barefoot Budd held a slight lead over Decker. Pulling up on Budd, Decker bumped the South African, who kept her balance and ran on. A second later Decker did it again, this time requiring Budd to stick out her leg to steady herself. Decker then tripped over Budd's extended calf and fell to the ground. Puica eventually won and Budd was not disqualified (she placed seventh). Decker refused to accept the fact that it had been an innocent accident, stoking the controversy over what she thought was an ugly, even intentional, foul.

The tenor and temper of the marathon could not have been more different. The only two runners in serious contention were Joan Benoit of the United States and Grete Waitz of Norway. Both had physical problems—Benoit was recovering from knee surgery and Waitz had developed a bad back—but both were serious, steady competitors, particularly Benoit, whom her coach described as having the "tremendous ability to blank out everything at the start of a race—heat, humidity, injury or pain." Benoit took an early and large lead, a move Waitz considered a mistake. The Norwegian waited for her to drop back, but Benoit never did; though Waitz began to catch up, it was too late. Benoit sailed into the stadium, for once nervous. "Listen," Benoit reassured herself as she finished the race. "Just look straight ahead, because if you don't you're probably going to faint."

243

American Carl Lewis, running at 28 miles per hour, pulls ahead in the 100-meter dash

CARL LEWIS

Sprinters have often been the most colorful and crowd-pleasing Olympic athletes. In 1984, competing in a city already full of stars of all kinds, the star sprinter was an independent-minded, self-contained young man named Carl Lewis. Lewis had been raised almost from birth to be a track-and-field performer. The son of two track coaches, he had hung around his parents' track club all his life. Lewis missed the 1980 games due to the boycott, but in 1984, having qualified for the 100- and 200-meter sprints, the long jump and the 4 X 100-meter relay, he was more than ready to attempt to equal Jesse Owens's victories in these same events.

The 100 meters Lewis won handily, flashing across the finish line at an estimated speed of 28 miles per hour. Two days later, he won the long jump with his first leap. After another leap he sat down, and to Lewis's astonishment the crowd, expecting him to take further jumps in an attempt to break Bob Beamon's world record, booed.

Lewis, who was conserving his energy for his next two races, explained the crowd's reaction: "I think the main problem was that the stadium was full of people who did not know much about track-and-field. Those who booed probably felt that they had paid to see a full six jumps. I think that many of them didn't understand that it only took one jump to win."

Lewis went on to win the 200-meter sprint and to take part in the winning relay race. According to Lewis the crowd began to catch on. After the 200, as he remembered, "When I won the gold medal, they roared and cheered and celebrated. You could hear people saying, 'Okay, I see what's going on here.'"

Following pages: American swimmers accept crowd's congratulations

     For all his apparent difficulties with Olympic spectators, Lewis keenly understood that great athletes had often doubled as great performers. As he once told fellow American sprinter Joe DeLoach about running victory laps, "Make sure you keep waving. Always give smiles. If you see somebody you know, give a little extra stare, because people notice that. They think that is nice."

     After his remarkable 1984 performance, Lewis planned to enter show business. But though he trained hard to be a singer, dancer and actor, stardom for Lewis remained on the track. Unlike past Olympians, for whom celebrity ended with closing ceremonies, by the late 1980s a talented and charismatic athlete could remain in the public spotlight both by continuing to compete and by reaping the commercial benefits of athletic and personal popularity.

     This Lewis did, appearing often on television and competing in two more Olympic Games. In Seoul in 1988 he repeated his victory in the long jump and was awarded first place in the 100-meter race after Canadian Ben Johnson was disqualified for using steroids. In 1992 in Barcelona Lewis again took the gold medal in the long jump and would have been competitive in the 100 meters had a virus not forced him withdraw.

     In 1984 Lewis predicted that he would go on to be a "respected entertainer." After twelve years in the spotlight Lewis had indeed become a star, though not, as he had planned, by performing on non-athletic stages. Lewis was a new breed of Olympian, one whose career was predicated on and perpetuated by his ability to continue being a great Olympic performer.

245

Korean crowd stands as Olympic torch is carried into stadium

Seoul
1988

Start of marathon, won by Gelindo Bordin (ITA)

On opening day of the Seoul Olympic Games, Korean crowds rose in a standing ovation as a thin, seventy-six-year-old man named Sohn Kee-Chung jogged enthusiastically into the stadium carrying the Olympic torch. To this crowd, proud of its preparations for a spectacular Olympics, Chung was the athlete most symbolic of the country's post–World War II accomplishments. During the prewar Berlin games, Korea had been overrun by Japan, and Chung, registered under the Japanese version of his name, Kitei Son, had been forced to compete under the Japanese flag. Now for the first time, Chung's country—and the world—were able to recognize that fifty-two-year-old gold-medal performance as one achieved by a citizen of Korea.

The Seoul games, though not the most controversial in Olympic history, were racked by a single, extremely important issue: the taking of performance-enhancing drugs. Despite the International Olympic Committee president's warning that "doping equals death," several winners had to be stripped of their medals when it was discovered that they had taken drugs. The most notable of these disqualifications was that of the Canadian sprinter Ben Johnson. A native of Jamaica, Johnson had dominated the world in the 100-meter sprint in the two years leading up to 1988. At Seoul he topped his previous world-record times, winning the 100 meters in 9.79 seconds. Though Johnson had repeatedly and vehemently denied drug use, a post-race test detected traces of steroids in his system. The entire athletic community was shocked, but none more so than Johnson's dismayed Canadian fans.

Carl Lewis, the gold medalist in 1984, was declared the winner of the race. He proceeded to claim a repeat

249

Ben Johnson (CAN; right), later disqualified, leads Carl Lewis (USA; center) in 100 meters

victory in the long jump but was narrowly beaten in the 200 meters by his teammate Joe DeLoach. In the 110-meter hurdles, Roger Kingdom (USA) easily repeated his Los Angeles win, but in a somewhat shocking development Edwin Moses not only lost the 400-meter hurdles but came in third.

It had been 28 years since Abebe Bikila became the first black African to win a gold medal. Since then, of course, African runners had either won or played an important role in many middle- and long-distance runs. In 1988 it was the Kenyans' turn to claim three important victories, two of which were won in upsets. The favorites in the 800-meter race were Said Aouita of Morocco and Peter Elliott of Great Britain. There were two Kenyans in the final, however, and they had a team strategy: Nixon Kiprotich, who had won the Kenyan national trials, set a terrifically fast pace in order to tire the field and put countryman Paul Ereng in a better position to come from behind and win. Aouita fell back early in the race. Elliott also faltered, and as the remaining runners headed toward the finish line, Ereng slipped almost unnoticed through the pack and won by 2 meters.

Britain's Steve Cram was favored to win the 1,500-meter race, but once again a virtually unknown Kenyan won. With half a lap left in the race, the surprising leader was Peter Rono. Though Cram, his teammate Peter Elliott and the German Jens-Peter Herold charged after him, Rono kept the lead and emerged as the second Kenyan upset-victor. On that same day a third Kenyan, John Ngugi, earned a gold medal, this time in the 5,000-meter race, though that commanding victory was no surprise at all for the five-time world cross-country champion.

American Jimmy Kim competes in men's judo

The women's track-and-field competitions, first introduced sixty years earlier, were as colorful and lively—if not more so—than the men's events. The American Florence Griffith-Joyner won gold medals in the 100- and 200-meter sprints as well as in the 4 X 100-meter relay, and her sister-in-law Jackie Joyner-Kersee double-medaled in the long jump and the heptathlon. Valerie Brisco-Hooks, the 400-meter champion in 1984, was unable to repeat and came in fourth behind the winner, Olga Bryzgina.

The 800 meters was a two-woman, one-country race, with Sigrun Wodars of East Germany defeating her long-time rival Christine Wachtel. The unfortunate Mary Decker again lost the 3,000-meter race. At that race's end, the eventual winner, Tatyana Samolenko, brushed past the pack, which did not include a trailing Decker, and won going away. The 1988 marathon was won by the great Portuguese runner Rosa Mota, who started her kick about 2 miles from the finish and won by a comfortable margin of 75 yards.

Though the American Matt Biondi won six medals in Seoul (golds in the 50 and 100 meters and the 4 X 200-meter freestyle and 4 X 100-medley relays, a silver in the 100-meter butterfly, and a bronze in the 200-meter freestyle), perhaps the most noteworthy performance in swimming was given by the Russian long-distance swimmer Vladimir Salnikov. The twenty-eight-year-old Salnikov, who had been the first man in history to swim 1,500 meters in less than 15 minutes and who had won three gold medals eight years earlier in Moscow, returned after missing the Los Angeles games to win his specialty once again.

251

Janet Evans (USA) collects three gold medals in freestyle and individual medley races

In women's swimming two names flashed most often on the results board: Janet Evans of the United States and the East German Kristin Otto. Evans was the dominant middle-distance swimmer of the games, gold medaling in the 400- and 800-meter races as well as the 400-meter individual medley. Otto was both a great freestyler and a great backstroker. She was victorious in the 100-meter freestyle, the 100-meter backstroke, the 4 X 100-meter freestyle relay and the 4 X 100-meter medley relay.

For the most part, the Koreans were fine hosts and fair officials—with the possible exception of the Korean boxing referees. In past games Korean boxers had lost controversial decisions, and to the Korean crowd history seemed to repeat itself when Korean bantamweight Byun Jong-Il lost a bout due to a head-butting call. After several similar incidents, the Korean fans became distressed and extremely angry, rushing the ring and attacking a winning fighter. Bad officiating, however, also *helped* Korean boxers. Park Si-hun, the light-middleweight champion, won so many obviously undeserved decisions that he became known as the "unbeatable Park Si-hun."

One of the great figures of the 1988 games was the weightlifter Naim Suleymanoglu. Until 1986 Suleymanoglu, a Bulgarian of Turkish descent, had lifted for Bulgaria. But after incurring much anti-Turkish discrimination, including an instance in which Suleymanoglu was forced to change the spelling of his name, he defected, and in 1988 the 5-foot weightlifter won a gold medal for Turkey. The Bulgarians lost not only this championship but also a number of other titles when it was discovered that practically the entire team was taking steroids.

Greg Barton (USA), double medalist in kayaking, takes 1,000-meter race by .005 second

GREG BARTON

The distinction is simple: those competing in Olympic Canadian canoe races kneel in the boat and paddle side to side with a one-bladed paddle, whereas kayakers sit with legs outstretched and propel their boats forward with a double-bladed paddle. Olympic kayaking debuted in 1936 with two events: the men's 1,000-meter pairs and the men's 1,000-meter singles. By 1988, the winning pairs time had been cut by 30 seconds and the singles time cut by almost a minute. Responsible, at least in part, for these records was a single man—Greg Barton, the first American to win an Olympic kayak event.

Barton, who was born with club feet, learned to paddle in the streams, lakes and rivers near his childhood Michigan home. He began to kayak competitively at the University of Michigan, and in the 1984 Olympics he won a bronze medal in the 1,000-meter singles. Barton had since undergone surgery on his feet, partially fusing his ankles, but fortunately the stiffness of his legs made little difference to his kayaking style.

Barton was favored to win the gold at Seoul, but the race was very close. As Barton looked up at the scoreboard after finishing the race, he saw his closest competitor's name, the Australian Grant Davies, listed as winner. American officials protested, however, and photo-finish film proved that Barton had won by 0.005 second, or one centimeter. An hour and a half later, Barton and teammate Norman Bellingham were victors in the men's 1,000-meter pairs, making Barton not only the first American gold medalist in kayaking but also the first double medalist in that sport.

Stylish Florence Griffith-Joyner (USA) celebrates Olympic victory

JACKIE JOYNER-KERSEE AND FLORENCE GRIFFITH-JOYNER

That two world-class athletes are related by marriage alone does not make them remarkable. Jackie Joyner-Kersee and Florence Griffith-Joyner's shared name may have been intriguing, but it was their skill, determination and style that singled out these sisters-in-law as stars of the 1988 games.

Both competed in organized sports of one sort or another as young girls. Jackie Joyner-Kersee, along with her brother Al, had been raised in East St. Louis, Illinois, in a poor neighborhood that both desperately longed to leave. As Al has said of their childhood, "I remember Jackie and me crying together in a back room in that house, swearing that we were going to make it. Make it out." Fortunately, both Joyners were superb and determined athletes and this became their exit ticket.

Al, who specialized in the triple jump, won a gold medal in 1984. Though the young Jackie Joyner had set a collegiate record in the long jump, she was perhaps better known at the time as a basketball player, starting as a varsity player each of the four years she attended U.C.L.A. Late in her college career this reputation began to change. One U.C.L.A. track coach, Bob Kersee, enthused about Joyner's track potential, convinced her to train for the heptathlon, for which she won the silver medal at the 1984 Los Angeles Olympics. Two years later the two married, and in 1988 Jackie Joyner-Kersee won both the long jump and the heptathlon at the Seoul games, scoring a remarkable 7,291 points, almost 1,000 points more than the score earned by the gold medalist who had bettered her in 1984.

Jackie Joyner-Kersee (USA) hurling metal javelin in world-record heptathlon performance

     Joyner-Kersee's sister-in-law began her career as Florence Griffith. Raised in a tough Los Angeles ghetto, Griffith began to display her obvious athletic ability as early as the age of seven, when she entered and won school races. In addition to her sheer talent, Griffith also brought to women's track-and-field a new and often surprising sense of style. From her mother, who was a seamstress, Griffith learned the sewing skills that enabled her to design and make her own colorful, wildly original running uniforms. (One of her best-known outfits was a lacy garment she laughingly described as an "athletic negligee.") Griffith's grandmother, who was a beautician, also contributed to the athlete's somewhat revolutionary appearance: Griffith customarily competed with brightly painted fingernails.

     Griffith attended college first at California State University, Northridge, where she too came under the tutelage of track coach Bob Kersee, and then at U.C.L.A., where Kersee had accepted a new job. In 1982 Griffith won the N.C.A.A. 200-meter championship.

     For all intents and purposes, 1984 seemed to mark the end of a distinguished—though in no way remarkable—career. Griffith competed in the 1984 games, winning a disappointing silver medal in the 200 meters. After that race she went into semi-retirement, working in a bank and as a hairdresser. Two years before the Seoul games, Griffith married Al Joyner, the brother of Jackie Joyner-Kersee, and returned to training. "It was time," Florence Griffith-Joyner said, "to run better or move on." And run better she did, breaking the world record in the 100 meters at the 1988 Olympic trials and winning one silver and three gold medals in the Olympic Games.

Uncurling from pike position, springboard-diving champion Greg Louganis (USA) hits head on board

GREG LOUGANIS

By the age of eleven Greg Louganis, an American of Samoan and European ancestry, began to gain the notice of the United States diving community. After winning the Junior Olympics in 1971 with a perfect score of 10, Louganis was approached by Dr. Sammy Lee, the 1948 and 1952 Olympic platform-diving champion, who wanted to coach the young diver. With no compensation other than personal satisfaction and a promise from Louganis to regularly clean the doctor's pool, Lee took Louganis on as a student.

Though still a very young, somewhat inexperienced diver, the sixteen-year-old Louganis made the Olympic team in 1976 and managed to capture second place in the platform event and seventh place in the springboard event. Like other American athletes, he did not compete in the 1980 Moscow games. By 1984, however, Greg Louganis had earned the almost undisputed distinction of being the best diver in the world, a reputation that was confirmed by his double gold medal in springboard and platform diving at the Los Angeles games, won by record-setting point margins.

Louganis was the favorite to win both medals again in 1988, but during the springboard preliminaries, while attempting a reverse 2½ pike, he hit his head on the diving board. After his cut was sutured and bandaged, Louganis, with a display of courage notably appreciated by spectators, competed in the springboard finals, scoring between 8 and 9 on the very dive he had been performing when he sustained the injury. After this victory, Louganis went on once again to win the platform-diving competition.

Following pages: Greg Louganis in mid-dive. American Steve Timmons leads volleyball team to victory.

REQUIRED STEPS OF DIVING 2½ PIKE OFF SPRINGBOARD

257

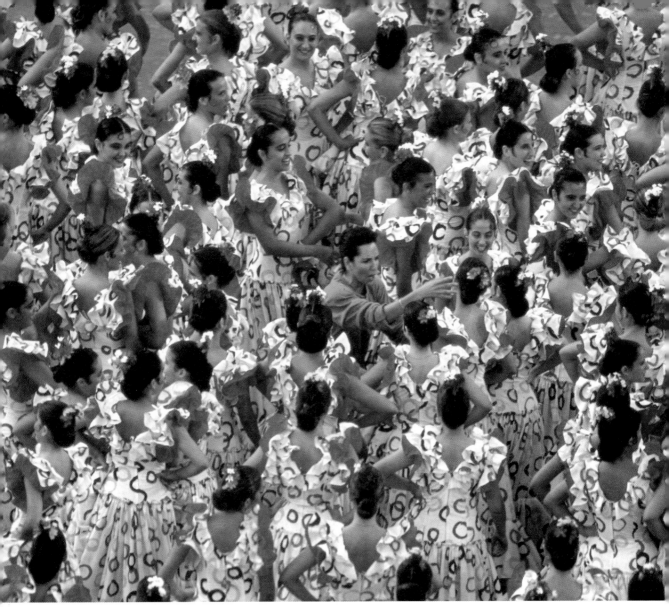

Barcelona
1992

Rider performing one of 36 movements "natural to a horse" in Olympic dressage

In 1992, two out of the era's three great Olympic sports superpowers no longer existed. Three years earlier, in 1989, the Soviet Union had lost dominance over its satellites. One of those, the German Democratic Republic, reunited with West Germany, marking the end of the legendary East German sports machine.

Only a year before the games, the U.S.S.R. itself fell apart, and Olympic officials made a last-minute decision to allow athletes from the former Soviet republics to compete under the banner of the Commonwealth of Independent States. As if these changes were not radical enough for one Olympics, for the first time the International Olympic Committee dropped its long-standing requirement that all athletes at the games be amateurs.

In many ways, there could have been no better venue for this almost brand-new set of games. Barcelona, itself coming slowly to life after being released from the repression of Francoism, put on an incredible show, more beautiful than the previous Seoul offering and more all-embracing than any Olympic Games over the previous ten years. In order to accommodate the Olympic activity, thirty miles of new roads were built, a new airport was constructed and the Montjuic stadium was renovated. Most spectacular of all, perhaps, was the Bernat Picornell natatorium, which clung to the side of a hill overlooking downtown Barcelona and gave those in the diving competition in particular the appearance of soaring in airy blue paradise.

Gracefully inaugurated by an archer lighting the stadium torch with a soaring flaming arrow, the opening ceremonies were symbolic of the 1992 Olympic Games themselves. Everything in Barcelona was sensational and

startling; nothing repeated the past. Over two billion people watched each televised event as they had watched the flight of the arrow: awed, expectant, and often amazed by the outcome of the athletic stories that unfolded.

In 1988, nineteen nations had medal winners in track-and-field. In 1992, even with athletes from the former Soviet Union still competing as a unit, this number increased to twenty-six. Additionally, the number of countries that had medal-winning athletes for the first time suggests how wide open the track-and-field competition was. Unfamiliar victors included Namibia, Qatar, Nigeria, the Bahamas and Lithuania.

Indeed, upsets in Barcelona often seemed to be standard fare. With Carl Lewis out of the sprint competition with a virus, for instance, the Americans Leroy Burrell and Dennis Mitchell were the favorites to win the race. But in the final the British sprinter Linford Christie, a man whose poor work habits had led others to describe him as an "athletic layabout," beat everyone at the start and pushed right on to win an upset victory. In the light of past Olympics, it would be expected that Christie would do well in the 200-meter race. But neither he nor the other favorite, Michael Johnson, even qualified for the final, which was won by the American Mike Marsh.

The 400-meter hurdles and the 400-meter flat races not only had unanticipated results, but to add to the drama they were won by Olympic village roommates. Even though Kevin Young of the United States stumbled over one of the first fences, he recovered and blew past Kriss Akabusi of Great Britain to win the 400-meter hurdles, in the process becoming the first man to break the 47-second barrier. In the 400-meter flat-race semifinal, the British

Olympic yachting, Flying Dutchman class

favorite Derek Redmond pulled a muscle early in the race and victory went—and in the final, too—to Young's room-mate Quincy Watts, who broke the tape as Redmond, helped by his father, limped his way toward the finish line.

Results of several of the field events were equally curious. Carl Lewis again won the long jump, but the great Russian pole-vaulter Sergei Bubka did not even qualify for the finals. The first three finishers in the shot put, Michael Stulce and Jim Doehring of the United States and Vjatcheslav Lykho of the Commonwealth of Independent States, had only that year returned to international competition after being suspended for using performance-enhancing drugs.

As if to reinforce the unpredictability of the 1992 results, the first and second finishers in the women's 10,000-meter race were two Africans representing countries at opposite geographical and political sides of the continent. First place in that event was taken by the Ethiopian runner Derartu Tulu, who became the first black African woman to win a gold medal in Olympic competition. Joining her in the victory lap was second-place finisher Elana Meyer, a white runner from South Africa, which was allowed to compete in 1992 after many years of being banned for its racial policies. "We both ran for Africa," Meyer said after the race. "I think we did that very well."

Like track-and-field, the swimming meets were also strangely atypical. With the disintegration of the muscle-bound East German women's team, the Hungarian triple-medalist Krisztina Egerzegi was said by many to represent the new spirit, if not soul, of women's swimming. At the same time, a new team at Barcelona seemed to have learned, or should one say disregarded, the lessons taught by East German training methods: Seemingly out of

nowhere, a group of unusually big, strong Chinese women achieved world-class status, winning a total of four gold medals in Barcelona in a variety of swimming events. Was this East Germany all over again? Many thought so. But because of Chinese restrictions on drug testing, the suspicions remained just that.

     One set of results that changed very little in 1992, however, was that of the gymnastics competition. Whatever their new team designation, the former Soviet gymnasts still had little credible competition. Indeed, the men's all-around champion Vitaly Scherbo completely outclassed his opponents and won six of the possible eight gold medals in men's gymnastics. In women's gymnastics the 1988 double-medalist Svetlana Boginskaya was upset not by any of the great Hungarian, Romanian or Chinese gymnasts, but by her own teammate, the slim Ukrainian Tatyana Gutsu.

     True to the spirit of the 1992 games, allowing professional athletes to compete had mixed consequences. Well-known professional Jennifer Capriati did win the women's singles tennis title, but though the men's field was stocked with the best players in the world, a lesser-known Swiss player, Marc Rosset, took the gold. There was, however, no possibility of upset in the basketball tournament, which was won, with almost laughable ease, by the so-called American "Dream Team" of N.B.A. professionals. At least one set of professional winners may have boded well for the future of Olympic competition: The badminton tournament, won by the Indonesians Susi Susanti and her fiancé, Allan Budi Kusma, was extremely popular and attracted worldwide television audiences. It was a new sport for a new Olympics.

TABLE TENNIS

At its inception the Olympic movement, patterned as it was after the ancient Greek competition, had been primarily Western by nature. Though running, jumping and throwing contests were not Western inventions, the particulars of those events, especially as constituted in the Olympic Games, certainly were. In spite of this European cast, not all Western-originated sports achieved their greatest popularity in the West. One of these Olympic events, invented by the Massachusetts-based Parker Brothers company, was "indoor" or table tennis. Though not included in the Olympic Games until 1988, table tennis had been extremely popular in Asia, particularly in Japan, China and Korea—countries that often invest national pride in their teams. Thus at the Seoul games, the host nation was delighted, and its closest neighbor shocked, when a member of the Korean men's team, Yoo Nam-kyu, won the gold medal. China fared better in the women's competition. Despite not sending their number-one player, He Zhili, for internal political reasons, the Chinese still easily won all three women's medals.

In Barcelona, the women's championship was again won by a Chinese player, the colorful nineteen-year-old Deng Yaping, who used a tennis grip rather than the traditional "pen-holder" style. The Chinese men, however, were not as successful. Many of their best players, such as Chen Xin-hua and Geng Lijuan, had emigrated to the West, and though the Chinese had convinced Olympic officials to bar these men from competition, their loss was felt on the Chinese team. Additionally, table tennis had gained great popularity in the West, and the best a Chinese player could place was third, behind gold-medalist Jan-Ove Waldner of Sweden and Phillipe Gatien of France.

GAIL DEVERS

There can be no nightmare more vivid and horrifying for an Olympic sprinter than to hear that doctors are considering amputating her feet. But for the American runner Gail Devers this was definitely no dream. In 1991, just a year away from the Barcelona games, the radiotherapy treatment she was receiving for a thyroid-gland problem caused her legs to swell out of control. The doctors delayed surgery, however, and slowly the swelling went down. Devers, who grew even more determined after her near tragedy, returned to training and, remarkably, qualified for the American Olympic team.

"You should never give up," Devers said, which she didn't, especially in the 100-meter final when, competing against the favored American Gwen Torrence, Merlene Ottey of Jamaica and Irina Privalova of the Commonwealth of Independent States, Devers scored an impressive, if not astonishing, first-place finish. Torrence could not believe the outcome and accused Devers of drug use. Torrence's anger, in whatever way misplaced, probably served her well in the 200-meter final, a race in which she breezed to a 21.81-second victory.

This was not the end of the drama in the shorter distance races, however. Devers was in the lead in the 100-meter hurdles and appeared close to capturing her second gold medal when she tripped so badly on the last hurdle that she fell to the ground and rolled across the finish line in fifth place. The victor in that race was a twenty-seven-year-old Greek runner named Paraskevi Patoulidou, whose win distinguished her as the first woman from her country ever to win a gold medal.

Right: USA defeats Italy in volleyball. Following pages: Michael Jordan. U.S. basketball team.

VOLLEYBALL

In 1896, a new sport called minonette was invented by a Y.M.C.A. athletic director in Holyoke, Massachusetts, as a less strenuous alternative to basketball. The game, renamed volleyball, became fairly popular, but mostly at the school gym, beach and backyard level—except in Japan, where it achieved the status of a craze after it was first introduced by American servicemen after World War II.

Volleyball was introduced as an Olympic sport in Tokyo in 1964. That year and in the next four Olympiads, the titles alternated back and forth between Japan and the Soviet Union, with Poland slipping one victory in. In 1984, however, the very strong American team won the Olympic tournament, a feat repeated in 1988.

Volleyball is also one of the few sports in which women achieved total and immediate equality on the Olympic program. As in the men's event, from 1964 onward teams from either Japan or the Soviet Union won practically all the gold medals in volleyball, the exception being a Chinese victory in 1984. Women's volleyball also had the reputation of producing extremely tough and well-trained athletes, particularly those from Japan.

The volleyball tournament, like much of the 1992 games, produced both expected and unanticipated results. The American men's players, after shaving their heads to protest poor refereeing in an earlier game, earned only a bronze medal. In the finals, the tactically aggressive team from the Netherlands was easily defeated by a taller and stronger Brazilian team. The women's title also changed hands in 1992, won by the Cubans, led by their dominating star, the twenty-four-year-old Mierya Luis.

269

Georgia Dome, site of 1996 Olympic basketball tournament

Atlanta
1996

ATLANTA 1996 ATLANTA 1996 Olympic badminton gained immediate popularity when it was inaugurated in 1992 ATLANTA 1996 ATLANTA 1996 ATLA

In the summer of 1996, more than 10,000 athletes from close to 200 countries will travel to Atlanta, Georgia, to participate in the Olympics (the 1896 Athens Olympiad saw only 311 competitors). As part of Olympic tradition, the athletes will be greeted by newly built, world-class facilities. The Atlanta Olympic Stadium, which can comfortably accommodate more than 85,000 people, will be the site of track-and-field events, while swimming will be held in the Georgia Tech Aquatic Center, baseball in Fulton County Stadium and basketball in Atlanta's Georgia Dome. Taking advantage of the unique regional geography, officials plan to hold a number of events in venues outside of Atlanta: from the canoeing slalom site at the Ocoee Whitewater Center in Tennessee to the yachting competition in Wassaw Sound near Savannah, Georgia.

Many of the athletes will compete in events as old as the ancient games themselves. Others will attempt to win in such new medal sports as beach volleyball and mountain biking. Some competitors will be eager amateurs; many will be seasoned professionals. With the addition of women's softball, soccer and judo, there will be more women competing than ever. All these changes, subtle or substantive, will contribute to the continuing evolution of the games. These additions and revisions will no doubt make the Atlanta games the most varied and exciting yet held. But the heart and soul of Olympic competition will not change. A hundred years of tradition will cycle ahead to the present, unfailingly fueling the dreams, and eventually the memories, of all the men and women whose names will enter the record books as the first participants of the second century of the modern Olympic Games.

The number of books written about the history and achievements of the Olympic Games is surprisingly small. Anchoring that relatively short list, however, is a volume whose breadth is so large that no one has yet attempted to better it. David Wallechinsky's *The Complete Book of the Olympics* (Viking, 1992), with its comprehensive statistics and well-researched stories, remains an unrivaled reference work for anyone eager to learn about the Olympics.

Other important texts on the Olympics include Dick Shaap's *An Illustrated History of the Olympics* (Knopf, 1963), which remains immensely readable. Connor, Dupuis and Morgan's *The Olympic Factbook* (Visible Ink Press, 1992) is a fine companion to Wallechinsky, and Kiernan and Daley's *The Story of the Olympic Games* (Lippincott, 1961), though dated in its language, is thoroughly enjoyable.

Page 157: Allsport/Hulton Deutsch. **Page 158:** Allsport/Hulton Deutsch. **Page 159:** Allsport/Hulton Deutsch. **Page 160 (left):** Allsport/Hulton Deutsch. **Page 161 (right):** Allsport/Hulton Deutsch. **Page 162 (left):** Allsport/Hulton Deutsch. **Page 162 (right):** Allsport/Hulton Deutsch. **Page 163:** Allsport/Hulton Deutsch. **Pages 164–165:** Allsport/Hulton Deutsch. **Page 166:** Allsport/Hulton Deutsch. **Page 167:** Allsport/Hulton Deutsch. **Page 168 (left):** Allsport/Hulton Deutsch. **Page 168 (right):** Allsport/Hulton Deutsch. **Page 169 (left):** Allsport/Hulton Deutsch. **Page 169 (right):** Allsport/Hulton Deutsch. **Page 170:** Allsport/Hulton Deutsch. **Page 171:** Allsport/Hulton Deutsch. **Page 172:** USOC. **Page 173:** USOC. **Pages 174–175:** USOC. **Page 176:** Allsport/Hulton Deutsch. **Page 177:** Allsport/Hulton Deutsch. **Page 178 (left):** Allsport/Hulton Deutsch. **Pages 178–179:** Allsport/Hulton Deutsch. **Page 179 (right):** Allsport/Hulton Deutsch. **Page 180:** Allsport/Hulton Deutsch. **Page 181:** Allsport/Hulton Deutsch. **Page 182:** USOC. **Page 183:** Allsport/Hulton Deutsch. **Page 184:** USOC. **Page 185:** USOC. **Page 186:** USOC. **Page 187:** USOC. **Page 188:** USOC. **Page 189:** Allsport/Hulton Deutsch. **Page 190:** USOC. **Page 191:** USOC. **Page 192 (left):** USOC. **Pages 192–193:** USOC. **Page 194:** Allsport/Hulton Deutsch. **Page 195:** Allsport/Hulton Deutsch. **Pages 196–197:** Allsport/Hulton Deutsch. **Page 198:** USOC. **Page 199:** Allsport. **Page 200:** USOC. **Page 201:** USOC. **Page 202 (left):** USOC. **Page 202 (right):** USOC. **Page 203 (left):** USOC. **Page 203 (right):** USOC. **Page 204:** USOC. **Page 205:** USOC. **Pages 206–207:** USOC. **Page 208:** Allsport/Hulton Deutsch/Tony Duffy. **Page 209:** USOC. **Page 210:** Allsport/Hulton Deutsch. **Page 211:** Allsport/Hulton Deutsch/Tony Duffy. **Page 212:** USOC. **Page 213:** USOC. **Pages 214–215:** Allsport/Hulton Deutsch. **Page 216:** Allsport/Hulton Deutsch/Tony Duffy. **Page 217:** Allsport/Hulton Deutsch/Tony Duffy. **Page 218 (left):** Allsport/Hulton Deutsch/Tony Duffy. **Pages 218–219:** Allsport. **Page 219 (right):** Allsport/Hulton Deutsch/Tony Duffy. **Page 220:** Allsport/Hulton Deutsch/Tony Duffy. **Page 221 (left):** Allsport/Hulton Deutsch/Tony Duffy. **Page 221 (right):** Allsport/Tony Duffy. **Page 222 (left):** Allsport/Hulton Deutsch. **Pages 222–223:** USOC. **Page 224:** Allsport/Don Morley. **Page 225:** Allsport/Tony Duffy. **Page 226:** Allsport/Hulton Deutsch. **Page 227:** USOC. **Page 228 (left):** Allsport/Tony Duffy. **Page 228 (right):** Allsport/Tony Duffy. **Page 229 (left):** Allsport/Tony Duffy. **Page 229 (right):** Allsport/Tony Duffy. **Page 230:** Allsport/Hulton Deutsch/Tony Duffy. **Page 231:** Allsport/Don Morley. **Page 232 (left):** Allsport/Tony Duffy. **Pages 232–233:** Allsport/Hulton Deutsch/Tony Duffy. **Page 233 (right):** Allsport/Tony Duffy. **Pages 234–235:** Allsport/Hulton Deutsch. **Page 236:** Allsport/Steve Powell. **Page 237:** Allsport/Hulton Deutsch. **Page 238 (left):** Allsport/Steve Powell. **Page 238 (right):** Allsport/Tony Duffy. **Page 239 (left):** Allsport/Hulton Deutsch/Steve Powell. **Page 239 (right):** Allpsport/Hulton Deutsch/Steve Powell. **Page 240 (left):** Allsport/David Cannon. **Page 240 (right):** Allsport/Steve Powell **Page 241:** Allsport/Hulton Deutsch/Tony Duffy. **Page 242 (left):** Allsport/Hulton Deutsch/Tony Duffy. **Pages 242–243:** Allsport/Steve Powell. **Page 243 (right):** USOC. **Pages 244–245:** Allsport/Hulton Deutsch/David Cannon. **Pages 246–247:** Allsport. **Page 248:** Allsport/Hulton Deutsch/Simon Bruty. **Page249:** Allsport/Hulton Deutsch/Yann Guichaoua. **Page 250:** Allsport/Hulton Deutsch. **Page 251:** Allsport/Hulton Deutsch/Billy Stickland. **Page 252:** Allsport/Hulton Deutsch/Simon Bruty. **Page 253:** Allsport/Mike Powell. **Page 254:** Allsport/Hulton Deutsch/Mike Powell. **Page 255:** Allsport/Tony Duffy. **Page 256 (left):** Allsport/Rich Clarkson. **Page 256 (right):** Allsport/Rich Clarkson. **Page 257 (left):** Allsport/Rich Clarkson. **Page 257 (right):** Allsport/Rich Clarkson. **Pages 258–259:** Allsport. **Pages 260–261:** Allsport. **Page 262:** Allsport/Hulton Deutsch/Simon Bruty. **Page 263:** Allsport/Hulton Deutsch/David Cannon. **Page 264:** Allsport/Hulton Deutsch/Simon Bruty. **Page 265:** Allsport/Nathan Bilow. **Pages 266–267:** Allsport/Hulton Deutsch/Pascal Rondeau. **Page 268 (top):** Allsport/James Meehan. **Page 268 (bottom):** Allsport/James Meehan. **Page 269 (left):** Allsport/Hulton Deutsch/Bernard Asset. **Page 269 (right):** Allsport/Hulton Deutsch/Bernard Asset. **Pages 270–271:** Allsport. **Page 272:** Allsport/Simon Bruty. **Page 273:** Allsport/Hulton Deutsch/Gary M. Prior. **Page 274:** Allsport/Hulton Deutsch/Mike Powell. **Page 275:** Allsport/Al Bello. **Page 276:** Allsport/Mike Powell. **Page 277:** Allsport/Hulton Deutsch/Richard Martin. **Page 280:** Allsport. **Page 281:** Allsport/Hulton Deutsch/Richard Martin. **Page 282:** Allsport/Hulton Deutsch/Pascal Rondeau. **Page 283:** Allsport/Hulton Deutsch/Mike Powell. **Page 286:** Allsport/Hulton Deutsch/Bob Martin. **Page 287:** Allsport/Hulton Deutsch/Pascal Rondeau. **Page 288:** Allsport/Hulton Deutsch/Gerard Vandystadt.

Page 274: Gintautas Umaras (URS), 1988. **Page 275:** Women's field hockey, U.S. Olympic Festival, 1995. **Page 276:** Beach volleyball, 1992. **Page 277:** Dan O'Brien (USA), 1992. **Page 280:** Stefan Edberg (SWE), 1984. **Page 281:** Handball, France vs. Romania, 1992. **Page 282:** Sychronized swimming, Camaron and Waldo (CAN), 1992. **Page 283:** Magic Johnson (USA), 1992. **Page 286:** Jay Hayes (USA), 1992. **Page 287:** Terry Bartlett (GBR), 1988. **Page 288:** Closing ceremony, 1992.

Page numbers in *italics* refer to illustrations.